Driftless
An Anthology of Voices from Where We Live

Edited by Sheree L. Greer and Stormy Stipe

Supported in part by an NEA Big Read grant
(NEA Big Read is a program of the National Endowment
for the Arts in partnership with Arts Midwest).

Copyright © 2025

All rights reserved. No part of this publication may be reproduced, distributed, or transmitted in any form or by any means, including photocopying, recording, digital scanning, or other electronic or mechanical methods, without the prior written permission of the publisher, except in the case of brief quotations embodied in critical reviews and certain other noncommercial uses permitted by copyright law. For permission requests or other information, please send correspondence to the following address:

Little Creek Press
5341 Sunny Ridge Road
Mineral Point, WI 53565

ORDERING INFORMATION
Quantity sales. Special discounts are available on quantity purchases by corporations, associations, and others. For details, contact info@littlecreekpress.com

Printed in the United States of America

Cataloging-in-Publication Data
Title: Driftless: An Anthology of Voices from Where We Live
Description: Mineral Point, WI Little Creek Press, 2025
Identifiers: LCCN: 2025912721 | ISBN: 978-1-967311-76-7
Classification: LITERARY COLLECTIONS / Essays
SOCIAL SCIENCE / Regional Studies
SOCIAL SCIENCE / LGBTQ+ Studies / General

Cover art: Heidi Dyas-McBeth
Editors: Sheree L. Greer, Stormy Stipe
Managing Editor: C. Kubasta

Book design by Little Creek Press

To the creatives of the Driftless—past, present, & future

CONTENTS

From The Editors

Stretch, Hold 1

Searching for Home 3

Artist Statement 9

Rock & Water

Kickapoo 12

Driftless Bedrock:
A Story of Limestone, Shale, & Sandstone 13

Butterfly Wings 30

The Power of Place 36

Sea Wall 42

Neighborhoods

Grant County 50

Inheritance 61

In The End 62

"This is Your Pasty":
Queer Domesticity in the Wisconsin Driftless 65

Sun Settle Down, Shadow's Galore:
A Love Letter to Nova 70

My grandmother was an unwanted child. 74

re-LIGHT 78

"Here-ness" in the Driftless 80

Great-Grandpa O'Brien 83

Wilma 84

Self-limiting 86

Self-talk 87

Flora & Fauna

To Those Everywhere Else 90

Bicycling the Driftless 94

River Valley Morning 99

Overheard at the Amish Shop in the Driftless 100

What the Light Is Hiding 101

Arms Full 113

Driftless Heart 115

What I Love About Where I Live,
Driftless Region 120

When the August 29 Dragonflies Rise 122

With Gratitude 124

About the Authors 126

FROM THE EDITORS

Stretch, Hold
Sheree L. Greer

I'm from the city. Born and raised in Milwaukee, Brew City blood pumps through these Wisconsin-born veins in ways that keep my head on a swivel, my spirit suspicious of too much silence. I haven't always thought about how much cityscapes shape a person or considered how little time I've spent in rural communities until visiting Mineral Point to teach and write at Shake Rag Alley Center for the Arts Writing Retreat, Mining Your Stories. I had never been to Mineral Point before coming for the retreat, and for the past four years, my stays in this small, sturdy town, where I feel still and restless at the same time, have been a mysterious tug and tow—a yearning for freedom, a movement toward home. Perhaps that's the spirit of the Driftless. Something defiant but familiar, the valleys, hillsides, and caves calling with open secrets.

I walk slower in the Driftless, the landscape a memory of highs and lows, the blue sky almost always full of cumulus clouds, heavy and cold as the snow I conveniently miss with my early summer visits. Whether a slap of foot against High Street or the crunch of gravel and snap of sticks hiking the Hill, I welcome the stretch in my calves and thighs, the lumbar ache of age holding me accountable to all my stories.

And I suppose I was looking for that feeling when I read the submissions to this anthology. I searched the poems and essays with intention, looking for pieces that had a time-traveling quality to them, a both/and that felt true to the valleys and crests of the Driftless, the bright open spaces and whispering shadows of the mines, the narratives of the people and the stories lodged between the stones.

Engaging with these selections is a lesson in the people, place, and taste—settlers and Indigenous, lush landscapes and flaky crusts—that hold the legends and lore of the Driftless, but it's also an invitation to create and hold space for the Driftless voices of the now.

Searching for Home
Stormy Stipe

What led my spouse and me to the Driftless Area was our search for home—over twenty years ago, when Jim and I were still wanderers. We were in our mid-thirties, having each recently finished our doctorates, and, excitingly enough, had both landed teaching positions in higher education. The problem was that they were over a thousand miles apart: mine in Winston-Salem, North Carolina, and his in Dubuque, Iowa. Jim and I were all too accustomed to going where our work and studies took us. I'd left Georgia to pursue degrees from Missouri to New York to Texas, while Jim had been lured in his early twenties from Canada to the U.S. by a graduate program in creative writing. We'd met in that program and, for six years, had shared the upper floor in a lovely brick duplex near Rice University in Houston. It had made us sad to dismantle that home with its makeshift furniture and dented pots and pans scavenged from the kitchens of aging parents no longer up for cooking. Now, to be splitting our belongings between my newly leased apartment in the South and his in the Midwest was upsetting, to say the least.

The summer before our long-distance living commenced, intent on making the most of our time together, we bought a Honda Civic, packed a tent, our sun hats, and a few books, and headed north. Our first stop was Jim's childhood home in Woodstock, Ontario. Jim's father, Phil, had died several months earlier, so we spent a week with his newly widowed mother, Irene ("Mum" to us), poring over photo albums late into the night at Mum's kitchen table. Then Jim and I said our goodbyes and continued north to Sudbury, Ontario, where Jim was born. There, on a whim, we knocked on the front door of his early childhood home, were invited in by the grown son of the couple who had bought the house from Jim's parents some thirty years earlier, and were asked to stay for dinner and the night, which we did. We were on a sojourn to visit some of the places where Jim's family had lived before his childhood with his parents in a white two-story house on a maple-lined street in Woodstock. It was a reflective time for us, and our quest was surely at least in part about our longing for a home together.

From Sudbury we drove north to the city Jim's mother was born and grew up in, Thunder Bay, where for the first time I met Lake Superior, which Mum's cousins called, simply, "the lake." We steamed ourselves in a sauna, then stood on the shore together before wading, hand in hand, into the shockingly cold water. Later, Mum's cousin Joy served us Finnish pancakes and loganberries. These were people who knew and loved that place deeply and made us feel at home there.

We experienced this again a few days later in Manitoba, when Jim's Uncle Don led us through thick weeds and saplings to the abandoned two-room schoolhouse he and Phil and their siblings had attended as children. It was where, he explained, Jim's father had found his love for learning, which had led him from the prairie farmlands of Manitoba eventually to Toronto for his university degree. Now in his eighties, Uncle Don pulled open the heavy wooden doors. "This is where it all started," he said. "We're so proud of Phil about his studies." I found the moment moving, for to see a place through the reminiscences of those whose lives have been formed by it is a gift.

After visiting Uncle Don and his wife, Aunt Jean, on their farm, Jim and I made a stop in Winnipeg, where we swatted clouds of mosquitoes away from our crepes at the open-air dining tables under the awnings of The Forks Market at the confluence of the Red and Assiniboine Rivers, and then we dropped back down into the United States, through North Dakota and Minnesota, south into Iowa, and down to Dubuque where we spent several days apartment hunting. Though Jim had been to Dubuque for his job interview several months earlier, I had never been there. Even before arriving, I had a grudge against the town—and, by association, all the Midwest—since it would be where my husband would live without me.

My mind was soon changed by the nature writer Kevin Koch, who, as chair of the department Jim would be joining at Loras College, invited us to join him and his family for dinner at his home. Even then, Kevin had already studied and written about the Driftless extensively. What better way to come to know this area than through conversation with Kevin and his wife, Dianne, who understand and love this place as deeply as anyone? Still, Kevin had his work cut out for him. I was sullen on the way to his house. Jim and I had been out looking at apartments, every one of which was, in my mind, sub-par because, again, my husband would be living in it without me.

Had I known the intensity of love a Driftless dweller has for this land, I might have understood how fascinated I would be by Kevin Koch's relationship to his beloved place. Kevin and Dianne's home was enchanting: the front porch that spoke endearingly to my Southern heart, the three framed school photos of their school-aged children on the living room wall (one of which hung upside down; when I remarked on it, Kevin and Dianne chuckled and shrugged), the fact that while Kevin heated the dinner rolls Dianne crossed the kitchen with a damp cloth in her hand and motioned for Jim and me to lift our arms from the table so she could wipe away the stickiness on it. It was a settled home, with all the warmth and humor of the home I wanted to have with Jim.

Over dinner, when I remarked on the beauty of learning about places through the people who love them and invited the Koches to tell us about this place, Kevin, despite having just wound a mouthful of saucy spaghetti onto it, dropped his fork and, with something like the enthusiasm of a tour guide, began to name the rivers, valleys, and bluffs, and to describe their beauty. The word *driftless*, he told us, refers to the absence of glacial drift, an area bypassed by a huge ancient washing over and flattening out, so instead of leaving behind silt and gravel, all that geological debris, what the last ice age left here is a diverse landscape of gullies, ravines, streams, deep river valleys, equally steep hills, ridges, and bluffs formed from limestone, dolomite, and sandstone, as well as gorgeous spring-fed waterfalls that are home to varied flora and fauna. This is the land through which, Kevin told us, he regularly rode his bicycle, and these were the rivers down which he and Dianne canoed with their kids. That evening, Kevin signed a copy of his book, *Skiing at Midnight: A Nature Journal from Dubuque County, Iowa*, and as he handed it to Jim and me, he said, "Welcome. There's a lot to love here."

Before that visit I think I'd morosely confused the word *driftless* with *drifter*, which brought to mind those alienated wanderers from Old English literature—the desolation of *The Wanderer* and *The Seafarer*, and even more apropos to my situation, *The Wife's Lament*. Now, some twenty years later, having moved here before long to live with Jim and having now myself a sometimes sticky table and all the warmth and humor I saw in the Koches' home, I've come to know and love this land, perhaps not as much as Kevin, but more than I ever thought I would.

Recently, while having my teeth cleaned by a woman who grew up in southern Wisconsin, I told her I'd grown up in south Georgia. "Oh," she said, with my mouth full of her hands and tools, "so after living here so long, does this feel more like home to you, or does Georgia still feel more like home?" I had time to ponder her question while she scraped vigorously at a molar. Finally, she removed the mirror and scaler and looked at me expectantly.

"Neither," I said. "I don't really feel at home anywhere. I feel like an outsider everywhere, and so," I said, seeing that she was inching her tools toward my mouth again, signifying that my time for speaking was up, "I try to access home inside me, like through meditation, which helps me be at home in the present, not any particular place."

She looked disappointed. She hadn't invited a discussion of mystical matters. Yet somehow the conversation—or her monologue, since I wasn't allowed another chance to speak until the cleaning was over—turned quickly to the hygienist's love of cleaning, not people's teeth, she explained, this was just a job, but her home. She described her vacuum cleaner to me—a really great one, she said—and explained her pleasure at how immediately it can make her home so clean and inviting.

While I didn't fully appreciate her love of a good vacuum cleaner, I did understand love of home. That, coupled with the pleasure of experiencing a place through the people who understand and love it most, inspired me to work on this anthology. To read the words of these Driftless dwellers, some of whom were born here, some of whom have been led here and have come to see themselves as part of this region (and to see it as part of themselves), and even some who express both alienation and belonging, well, for me there is no more delightful way to further my understanding of this place and how and why it is home to its inhabitants. The works in this anthology have inspired me to consider that the home I find when I turn inward on my meditation cushion might also be accessible in the way these writers seem to find it: through hikes, explorations, studies, and a sacred reverence for this place. As the poet Gary Snyder put it, "Nature is not a place to visit. It is home." As an inhabitant of the Driftless Area, I feel a bit closer to home after having read the testimonies of wonder and insight and reverent pondering collected here.

Artist Statement

Heidi Dyas-McBeth

Designing the cover art for *Where We Live* has been a deeply personal project. The landscapes where I grew up—and where I now live—are integral parts of my identity. Over the past five years, I've nurtured a growing fascination with how the Earth was formed, how natural features influence migration and settlement, and how the land can shape creativity, compassion, and a sense of connection.

The initial inspiration for the cover design came from the shape of the Driftless Area's boundaries, which resemble a butterfly or moth chrysalis. Over time, that image evolved into a symbol of transformation—of shedding one state of being to embrace another. In that sense, this project became biographical: My own emergence as an artist has been deeply nurtured by the landscape and the community of the Driftless region.

Unlike most of the Midwest, the Driftless was never flattened by glaciers. Instead, its character was carved slowly by erosion, revealing millions of years of geologic history. The ridges and river valleys of this land guide and challenge us, exposing layers of bedrock that tell stories of ancient transformation—stories I try to echo in my work.

Now in my sixties, I identify as an Earthling and a visual artist while also embracing my roles as a partner, mother, grandparent, daughter, sister, and friend. My journey began in the wide-open landscapes of Nebraska, followed by time in the Shawnee National Forest of southern Illinois, before settling in the Driftless Area in 1996. My artistic practice includes drawing, collage, and mosaic, and since 2019, a revived sketchbook habit has reconnected me to both art and place. Exploring the riches of where I live continues to inspire and inform my work.

SECTION ONE
Rock & Water

Kickapoo

Jesse Lee Kercheval

I stand in the middle of a field in the Driftless and the open space makes me a letter. Me plus you a word. Us plus four sandhill cranes a sentence walking forward on skinny bent legs. I stand in the middle of the West Fork of the Kickapoo and I am, at the very least, an exclamation point—emphasizing the fast-flowing water. Add the yellow canoe I tipped out of, racing down the river, and there is the start—or end—of a sentence. The day an alphabet in a line above the blackboard in a classroom. Lines: vertical, horizontal, curved—the odd dot. A convenience store of language. But it's the space around the letters gives that shape to the words. Swimmers coordinate their strokes, and inside the crook of an elbow, water ballet is born. *Existence makes a thing useful. Nonexistence makes it work.* The hollow in our hearts makes room for all the blood.

Driftless Bedrock: A Story of Limestone, Shale, & Sandstone

Kevin Koch, Dale Easley, and Curt Meine

Introduction

I once drove a job candidate around my niche of the Driftless to give her a sense of the landscape. It was February, probably not the best time to entice a warm-climate applicant. In a forested section of town, I slowed down, motioned, and said that I liked how I could see deeply into the woods at this time of year.

"To see what?" she panned. "The *rocks*?"

Needless to say, the candidate didn't move up any notches, in my estimation.

Our Driftless neighbors will use various means to describe our landscape. Hilly, because the glaciers missed us (or the later ones did, at the Driftless edges). Steep ravines. Winding creek-valley roads. Oak-hickory prairie savannas. Contoured farm fields. Trout fishing.

Geologists will add their own lingo and descriptors. The Paleozoic Plateau, in which there are few true hills but a prevailing plain that is everywhere downcut so that water races to the streams and rivers and ultimately to the Mississippi. Lands that the great ice never overlaid with glacial drift—the boulders, gravel, sand, and dust that overtops our glaciated neighbors' bedrock.

For some of us, though—even the non-geologists among us—the Driftless Area means bedrock, the bones of the earth sticking out in sheer three- and four-hundred-foot river bluffs or protruding in small hillside patches like scabby knees. Forget the loamy soils that give easy bedding to plant roots. Give us something hard instead, something unspeakingly solid.

It's not simply the rocks themselves but the way that bedrock forms our foundation. In the Driftless, three types of bedrock predominate, along with their particular allures: limestone feeds our sense of the mysterious; sandstone tells a silent story of ancient seabeds and upland dunes, teaching us to embrace the flow of time; shale points to transitions in climate and sea levels and in our very lives.

And so three of us set out to find the story in the rocks most prevalent to where we live: Kevin in the limestones of northeast Iowa and the Upper Mississippi River corridor, Curt in the sandstones of southwest Wisconsin, Dale in the shales that buffer between them.

It's easy, if not shortsighted, to view the meaning of flatland soil as that which gives birth handily to corn and soybeans. It takes some excavating to wrestle meaning out of the bedrock.

Limestone

Maybe it's the river bluffs near Prairie du Chien, Wisconsin, rising four hundred feet from either side of the Mississippi so steeply that exposed, sheer limestone cliffs dot yellow-tan against the forested hills. Or maybe this: I am driving a stream-bottom highway in northeast Iowa when the road bends around a limestone tower cleaved from its mother bedrock.

Or even an abandoned limestone quarry, a defacement of the landscape, like Horseshoe Bluff at Dubuque's Mines of Spain, where two hundred fifty feet of sheer dynamited rock wall presents itself as a beautiful scar. Oaks line the top of the quarry, while cedars sprout precariously from crevices and ledges. A thin soil and quaking aspens are slowly reclaiming the quarry floor.

Or maybe it's limestone foundations, like the yellow-buffed rock that has supported my Dubuque house for over a hundred years. Or the thirty-foot castellated limestone monument that encircles the grave of Julien Dubuque, for whom our city is named. The monument sits on a prominent bluff overlooking the Mississippi River. I go there every solstice and equinox to watch the sun rise over the river bluffs.

Whatever the cause, place, or reason, limestone is my bedrock.

Here in the Driftless, the oldest limestone was laid down in shallow equatorial, Ordovician seas four hundred fifty million years ago. The lime derives from the shells of dead sea creatures piling up on the sediment-laden sea floors. Time and weight pressed the whole concoction into rock. Fossils from these warm, shallow seas populate Driftless limestone. Gastropods were prototypes of today's snails. Trilobites resemble fat, shelled millipedes, and cephalopod fossils look like tiny party hats that once sat atop squid-like creatures. Coral fossils masquerade as tiny bits of honeycomb.

A later layering of Niagara limestone formed during the Silurian Age three hundred million years ago. Niagara limestone caps our natural Driftless mounds— Sinsinawa, Platteville, Belmont, and Blue Mounds—that poke two hundred feet or more above the prevailing landscape, receding eastward from the Mississippi River like stepping-stones for the gods. When I return from a trip away, I know I'm home when the limestone mounds come into view.

Geologists will speak more accurately of how and when Driftless limestone formed. But what they won't quite explain is that limestone is magical. Surface bedrock limestone in the Driftless produces a karst topography flush with sinkholes, caves, rock shelters, and algific talus slopes that play tricks with time and shape. When limestone lies just under the soil surface, water will pool

15

in the slightest indentations, seep through the tiniest of vertical cracks, widen those fissures, find a hard floor (often shale), and dissolve a horizontal pathway to form an underground stream. When limestone beneath the soil weakens, the surface may collapse into a sinkhole, a roundish slump feeding directly into the underground flow. One evening, a part of my niece's yard in Dubuque dropped away, nearly taking the backyard deck and pool with it. Streets, side yards, and parked cars occasionally disappear into the ground overnight in my town, often after torrential downpours.

Lateral flowing, underground streams produce Driftless caves, expanding their caverns as they dissolve the limestone. Cracks in the limestone ceilings—known as lifelines—feed the underground streams with nearly continuously dripping water. Having dissolved calcium carbonate in its slow downward trek through the overhead bedrock, groundwater sheds the mineral as it drips from the ceilings or slides down the cave walls. The result is a mineral "ice" or "glass" hanging down from the cave ceiling (stalactites), growing on the splashed-upon floor (stalagmites), or sheening in ripple flows against the rock. The oils from a single touch of human skin can stop the growth of a formation, putting the brakes on a stalactite that otherwise may have lengthened by a centimeter per century. The formations take on fantastical shapes, unseen by the human eye until recent centuries and even now only by electric light during cave tour hours.

Fissures can also lead to mineral formation, like the milky white quartz compacted into chert that brightens a band of limestone. Such spaces remind us of our own interior beauty and mystery.

In some places the cave ceilings have collapsed over time, leaving just the cave walls protected by curved overhangs (the ceiling remnants). These are rock shelters used long ago by Indigenous peoples for winter shelter. Or the collapsed cave may expose small feeder side caves. Each winter I explore the ice cave at Lost Canyon, where dripping water and unpredictable air currents produce seasonal ice sculptures. In various winters, I have discovered leg tendons, skull-faced statuettes, and—I kid you not—a Holy Family Nativity scene in the ice formations. There's no need to pilgrimage there, however, as the figures melt away each spring and form again with new designs each winter.

The ice cave is just above the valley floor, recognizable in winter by a thick, banded frost above the cave mouth. This is where the earth breathes.

Hills of fractured limestone are called algific talus slopes, where warm summer air flows over last winter's ice in the deep recesses, then cools and vents like air conditioning at the base. Here, the microclimate coolness provides a haven to relic species hanging on from the end of the ice age, with fern-like monkshood parading purple flowers and tiny Pleistocene snails seeking shelter from a changing climate.

In winter, the process is reversed. Warm air rises from the upper vents while cold air enters from the bottom and freezes a new pool to refrigerate next summer's heat. In winter I have tossed a handful of fresh snow across an upper vent and watched it puff into the air like confetti. This, too, is where the earth breathes.

If the water disappears into limestone, it must emerge again, perhaps miles away, another kind of magic. Driftless limestone produces a wealth of springs and clear, cold trout streams.

Where a cave stream emerges on a vertical rock face, a waterfall, big or small, will result. On the Upper Iowa River, small, splashing waterfalls will cool a summer's kayak outing. At Decorah's Dunning Spring, a full-grown stream gushes from limestone walls as if Moses had tapped the rock to quench the thirst of his people. Or artesian springs may gush up from the floor of a pond or stream, forced to the surface by underground pressure. At Iowa's Backbone State Park, I've watched pool bottoms swirl in tempests as artesian flows burble up through the sand.

Humans arrived in the Driftless about twelve thousand years ago, almost within the shadows of the continental Wisconsinan glaciers. Driftless limestone gave them winter protection in caves and rock shelters. The cold, clear spring waters that accompany limestone provided fish and attracted game.

Driftless land peoples utilized—or exploited—the bedrock for the wealth found in lead and, later, zinc found in the limestone fissures. The same cracks through the limestone that let water trickle down from above also allowed long-ago briny subterranean waters to boil up through the rock like a bad case of indigestion, leading to the formation of lead. Each burst left behind a bit of mineral that eventually became lead deposits. Native Americans had mined lead for centuries before the mineral attracted the first wave of Euro-American immigrants.

Julien Dubuque mined lead beginning in 1788 after receiving permission from the Meskwaki. He died in 1820 and was buried next to the Meskwaki chief, but later immigrants mined until around the 1860s, long after the Meskwaki had been forcibly removed. At the Mines of Spain south of Dubuque, I take an annual winter hike (often with students) up through the limestone bluffs to an off-trail river bluff where hundreds of small lead mine pits have lain abandoned for one hundred fifty years while the forest regrew around them. This is another beautiful scar.

I am the product of where I live. Driftless limestone becomes me.

I am fissured by age lines around my eyes and the folds above my brows. My arms and legs have scars that have softened over time and become the stuff of stories. Within me lies the beauty of quartzite and the poison of lead. I am a warm, shallow sea transforming the detritus of life.

In summer I vent coolness at my sides; in winter I puff a warm stream of air against the cold. My mind grows still. The Earth breathes.

I am the darkness of a cave in a Driftless karst landscape. Water has dissolved and tunneled my bedrock. Distant drippings plink into a chilled pool of water, and stalactites grow in my recesses. Underground streams run undetected within me.

Somewhere far distant on the landscape, my stillness pours out on a limestone cliff.

—Kevin

Shale

Every fall semester before I retired, I took my Environmental Geology class to a roadcut ten miles into Wisconsin along the Highway 151 arterial connecting Dubuque to Madison. The limestone roadcut here is among the deepest in Wisconsin. But if one drives past the roadcut to the bottom of the valley, sandstone finally peeks out at a natural outcrop, the nearest visible sandstone layer in the Dubuque area.

The yellow sandstone at the bottom preserves the markings of an old sand dune deposited on ancient land. Above it lies a thin line of greenish shale formed where there was little oxygen to turn the green iron-bearing minerals red. And above the shale are additional sandstone and limestone layers, bearing evidence that they formed beneath ancient seas.

Like a pile of unopened mail, the oldest is on the bottom. And if we read it forward in time, we can see the land being submerged—a transgressive sequence.

The shale marks the beginning of a new chapter. The muddy clay and silt are finally settling from the ocean's water as it deepens and stills, encroaching on the land.

Such is the transition in which I find myself, having retired last year. I need to slow down, make no quick decisions out of anxiety, seek clarity and new life, before writing the next chapter.

From the outcrop, we drive a mile back toward Dubuque, park, again climb from our school vans, and hike uphill along the roadcut.

When the road was widened into four lanes in 1982, the roadbed was excavated through the overlying limestone and loess—glacial dust forming a much younger skin atop the hills—then down through a thick shale layer and into another limestone layer. The old blast holes drilled through the rock are still visible, though I have convinced a few gullible students that those are from ancient worms. Shame on me.

As we hike along the roadside, trucks race past at seventy miles per hour, often drowning out my voice. We climb over concrete barriers by the roadside, clamber through the brush, and get close to seeps and drips of water and mossy rocks.

At first glance, the seeps seem random. The challenge is getting students to slow down, look, and see relationships. And, of course, to stop using their cell phone except for photos.

Slowing down, looking for the details, is the way a writer seeks to illuminate the universal. And the way a geologist seeks to understand natural processes.

Across the road, the sunny side of the roadcut is drier. Less vegetation masks the rock layers, and a wider perspective helps the students clarify their thinking. Now clearly visible, a dark band runs between the layers, the shale between layers of limestone. That shale layer is the key to understanding the seeps of water right in front of them.

As rain falls on the ground surface above the road cut, it infiltrates and moves downward through the pore space of the soil and loess, into vertical fractures in the limestone, until its way is blocked by the low permeability of underlying layers, especially shale. At that point, groundwater moves horizontally along bedding planes, the flat surfaces separating layers of sedimentary rock. At the roadcut, the water seeps out.

At several seeps, mosses have grown from the shale downward, a green marker of persistent wetness. Water clings to the surfaces or drips off unevenly weathered protrusions. A tiny wetland. In winter, this water forms curtains of ice, a frozen waterfall that even the drivers passing by at seventy miles per hour can appreciate.

For my students, this is one of their first true geologic outings. In much of the Midwest, cars pass through miles of flat land and corn or beans, punctuated randomly with the seemingly out-of-place glacial erratic—a big boulder alongside the road, decorated with graffiti and flags. The occasional roadcut gives a glimpse of what lies beneath. Here in the Driftless Area, my students encounter streams that have spent millennia cutting through the rock layers, leaving limestone bluffs towering above the deeply incised streams.

But always, the shale is there, too. Marking the transgressions and regressions—the transitions—and the time of settling and clarification.

On a bluff face, the shale layer is an indentation, a wrinkle that shows the years of erosion. The bones of the limestone stick out, forming beautiful towers and cliffs.

But the shale recedes. It looks weak. Crumbly. It reflects little light. Plant seeds easily get their start there, their roots penetrating. In the Driftless, a line of cedars often marks the shale layer, part of the green glacier that has swept across what few remnants of prairie remain in the area, as fire no longer melts them back.

Another transition for another time.

As the ancient waters deepened and slowed, sunlight penetrated the clearing water, and new life grew. When those organisms died, they, too, settled to the ocean's bottom and were layered with the mud.

When something dies, chances are that it will leave this world without a trace. If its body remains on the ground surface, it becomes food for others and breaks apart under the forces of decomposition and erosion.

Dust to dust.

But if that creature is buried quickly, the chance that it will be someday remembered radically increases. As the weight atop the dead creatures accumulates, the layers of mud and death are compressed into shale. Some of those organisms are preserved as fossils, letters written on the shale. A history of past life.

Young people are often fascinated by dinosaur fossils, but these are more like a young adult book—romantic, showy, easy to grasp. An earlier classic is the Burgess Shale, a Cambrian deposit over five hundred million years old in which an abundance of creatures were preserved—mostly tiny things but the ancient ancestors of forms of life to follow.

The sequel to the Cambrian Period was the Ordovician Period. The Driftless Area has a famous fossil-rich outcrop of the Ordovician-age Maquoketa Group along the Heritage Trail near Graf, Iowa. In those layers of alternating limestone and shale are the fossils of the early, fierce ocean predators—squid and octopus and chambered nautilus—and smaller graptolites. The graptolite fossils got their name because they appear like pencil marks written in the rock.

Small traces of an ancient past.

As a young scientist, I was surprisingly poor at noticing details. I liked the big theories, like plate tectonics, and the computer models and their generated images. I sometimes wrote computer programs that generated solutions that were physically impossible—negative concentrations, like some sort of black hole that sucks out pollution. That would solve some problems! I wish.

Much later, I realized that I was unlikely to make any significant research breakthrough. But I could work on communicating scientific ideas to non-scientists, especially through storytelling. Working with an English professor-coach, I began to see how murky my thinking was, how often I failed to observe clearly, a sort of noetic disorder common to those from dysfunctional families.

Sir Ken Robinson said that for many academics, their bodies were for taking their heads to meetings. We live in our heads—that's what a noetic disorder is. But good writing is embodied. Grounded. Specific. We dig through the generalities and cliches to get to something deeper.

For me, working on writing was like going to therapy.

The mud needed to settle out for me to begin to see more clearly. And for new life to thrive.

—Dale

Sandstone

> One hundred and eighty billion spins, more or less,
>
> days and nights flowing in and out of each other
>
> over ancient plateaus, former flats rain-rendered
>
> into valleys, ledges, and ridges. Add one more day.
>
> A few grains of Tunnel City sandstone loosen and
>
> slip an inch under raindrop pelt and squirrel heel,
>
> an iota of time marking contours of bluff and coulee,
>
> disturbing occasional fossil trilobites and gastropods,
>
> yellow sands lodged in vanquished mammoth footfalls,
>
> where the People welcomed dawning suns across millennia,
>
> moved from the big river to up-valley hollows and back again.
>
> Just now, a momentary celebration, as cranes return and remind.

I am still learning my layers. It takes time. My backyard bluff, on the east coast of the Driftless, holds one hundred and twenty feet and ten million years of ancient sands compressed into stone. I make that uphill hike in five minutes. If I walk on a little further, to the next bluff, I can add another sixty-five feet and twenty million years. When I am in a hurry to get to the overlook, I overlook the worlds underfoot.

But when I slow myself down, I can try to decipher the sandstone stories of the exposed strata along the way. A thick seam, bright white-yellow, smooth and coherent, conjures calm and steady seas. Above that, a series of more finely laminated layers, beige with greenish stain, suggests scummy saltwater shallows. Above that, a cross-bed of coarser buff grain, pitched at a twenty-degree angle, marks a dune or sandbar locked in place. Above that, a zone of amber stone, pocked, fractured, and crumbly, has a hard time holding itself together. And above that, on top, a thin rim of soil grows prairie dropseed and leadplant, butterfly weed, and puccoon.

I don't know if I am hearing the stories right. I am still learning my layers, seeking to understand transitions and transgressions, forces and fluxes. I am still trying to know their realities, of resistance through cementing and reinvention through weathering. These sandstone layers stretch across the Midwest, the lenses of rock thinning and thickening and thinning, differing from and dovetailing into one another. Beyond the Driftless, the sandstones remain mostly hidden, bearing the burden of more recent glacial deposits, thick soils, and surface waters on their broad, flat back. But within the Driftless, the currents of change, of shifting climate, continents, and chemistry, are apparent. They appear in the stone. They outcrop and cannot be avoided or ignored. Here we can look ourselves in the rock face.

A few miles to the east of my backyard, the Wisconsin River enters the Driftless. The river commences up north in springs, wetlands, and lakes, draining the hard, old igneous and metamorphic rocks of the Precambrian shield. It begins its journey south and crosses the terminal moraine of the last glacier near Merrill. It flows through older glacial deposits until it reaches Wisconsin Rapids. There it enters the sand plain that was the bed of glacial Lake Wisconsin until (17,400 years ago) the lake drained itself and carved through the sandstones at Wisconsin Dells. The seven-mile Dells gorge cuts through strata somewhat older than those of my backyard. The river then makes its wide hairpin turn around the Precambrian Baraboo Hills. It crosses back again across the terminal moraine at what is now the site of the power dam at Prairie du Sac, the last dam on the river. From then on, the Wisconsin River wends westward into and through the Driftless toward its confluence with the Mississippi at Wyalusing.

The river leaves Sauk Prairie and enters the Driftless Area through two sentinel bluffs on either side of its wide floodplain.

Along its south side, the Wisconsin River first meets Black Hawk Ridge, a two-mile long, four-hundred-foot-high rampart. The bulk of the bluff is sandstone capped by more resistant dolomite, but most of the rock is hidden under a mantle of restored prairie, oak savanna, and varied woods. It was here in 1832 that the Battle of Wisconsin Heights unfolded. The Sauk leader Black Hawk (*Mahkate:wi-meši-ke:hke:hkwa*) and his warriors, badly outnumbered, took their high ground atop the sandstone and dolomite. They held off the U.S. Army and state militia forces long enough for their people, the "British Band" of Sauk, Meskwaki (Fox), and Kickapoo, to escape across the Wisconsin, with the intent of heading west toward the Mississippi River and finding refuge on its far side. The beleaguered band, starving and scattered, traversed the heart of the Driftless. The land's confounding topography of sandstone-derived ridges and valleys provided cover through their desperate flight. But the rock could not protect them when they came to the Mississippi at the mouth of the Bad Axe

River. There, under the looming sandstone bulk of Battle Bluff, militia forces massacred the people.

Along its north side, the Wisconsin River's main channel crosses its floodplain beyond Black Hawk Ridge and comes to Ferry Bluff. Though not quite as high as Black Hawk Ridge, Ferry Bluff rises more dramatically from the river. A designated state natural area, it serves as a gateway into the Driftless Area and is a popular destination for hikers, paddlers, and birders. If you follow the trail up the bluff, you'll take a sedimental journey through Cambrian bedrock. The trailhead begins in brownish-yellow Wonewoc sandstone, which just pokes out above the river. Climb the bluff's three hundred forty feet, and you will rise through a thick layer of green-tinted Tunnel City sandstone, brighter St. Lawrence dolomitic siltstone, and pale-yellow Jordan sandstone. If you are ambitious and continue to the blufftop, you leave the late Cambrian and ascend into the early Ordovician Period via the light brown Oneota dolomite. There are no trail markers to guide you in your time traveling. You just have to slow down, pay attention, and learn your layers as you walk on.

Thus oriented at the eastern portal of the Driftless, along the Lower Wisconsin River that rolls ninety miles unimpeded to the Mississippi, one can calibrate one's position within the stack of sedimentary beds. Heading to Galena? You'll find scant sandstone there. Mostly younger limestones, dolostones, and shale. Heading to the Upper Iowa River? Not much sandstone at the surface in northeast Iowa. But the Jordan and Wonewoc formations reach across the Mississippi, and the yet older Eau Claire and Mount Simon sandstones appear in the Upper Iowa's palisade walls. To Grandad Bluff in La Crosse, and you'll find the same layers as Ferry Bluff's—

Wonewoc, Tunnel City, St. Lawrence, and Jordan—but capped there by Shakopee dolomite.

These sandstones of western Wisconsin hold other layers of story, ever being laid down. They largely escaped the wave of lead and zinc mining that came to their younger dolomitic neighbors in the 1800s. The steep contours of sandstone coulees were none too friendly to new European settler farmers who unwisely plowed them too straight and too far upslope. As erosion washed away the vulnerable topsoil, a revolution in soil conservation and watershed restoration came, starting in the 1930s.

Then, in the early 2000s, the ancient sand grains themselves brought modern forces of exploitation to bear. Having tumbled about Cambrian seas, they lost their edge and became too round for their own good. The burgeoning fracking industry needed particular grains of sand to help prop open fractured veins in gas- and oil-bearing shales in Pennsylvania and North Dakota. They found them in ideal form—round, resistant, pure quartz—in the St. Peter, Jordan, Wonewoc, and Mount Simon formations of western Wisconsin and Minnesota. Industrial machinery exposed, crushed, cleaned, and transported Driftless sandstones that glaciers could never touch. Until, after a decade, it became cheaper to dig into the Hickory Sandstone in central Texas.

The frac sand boom serves as a reminder. It's easy to focus on the visible faces of sandstone—the dramatic outcrops, quarry cuts, and exposed bluff sides that draw the eye. But then there are the subterranean layers that we don't see. The porous sandstones that hold and yield our life-giving groundwater and that cool and recharge our surface streams. Aquifers that emerge as springs and serve as passageways for the spirits. Sandstone caves whose walls host Native petroglyphs and pictographs and echo yet with stories told by torchlight.

I am still learning my layers and always need to remember that much of their reality resides below ground, hidden from view but holding us up, their rounded granules propping open our imaginations. I can't anticipate all the stories they may tell, but I can appreciate their potential for revelation. In hardened strata of ancient dunes and seabeds, as much as in the broad beaches of the present, we can strive with William Blake "To see a World in a Grain of Sand / And a Heaven in a Wild Flower / Hold Infinity in the palm of your hand / And Eternity in an hour."

It is time to walk the bluffs again, every footfall an opportunity to see oneself in the sandstones, to join in their ways of change, and to flow with them into the future.

—Curt

Conclusion

That long-ago job candidate who saw only "rocks" in the wintertime woods was shortsighted indeed. Kudos, I suppose, that she *did* see the rocks. But she didn't see *into* them, didn't know their story of formation and revelation, couldn't understand how our stories here in the Driftless derive from the bedrock and are imprinted in the bedrock. She seemed unaware that the apparent solidity and timelessness of rock is, in reality, merely a snapshot of time, a finite point among endless cycles of being built up and worn down and built up again. Just like all of us.

Perhaps she might have come to understand all this had she been offered the job, accepted the job, settled down in the Driftless, and joined us in the bedrock.

Butterfly Wings
Coleman

Synopsis

In the 1920s and 1930s, a dying Cornish mining village (Mineral Point, "the town where Wisconsin began") is rescued by two men, forever changing the character of the town and forging a cherished historic legacy.

BUTTERFLY WINGS

> *Sounds of nature.*
> *Robert Neal, thirties, stands alone on a bare stage.*

ROBERT NEAL

Close your eyes.

No. Seriously. Close your eyes.

You're dreaming. Or not. It doesn't matter. Illusion. Reality. They are all the same. This is theatre, after all. It's supposed to be an illusion.

One of us is a ghost. I'll give you a hint. It isn't you.

You're dreaming you're in a modest-sized theatre. There is a lone man on stage. That man is me. You are surrounded by strangers. That's okay. They are people more or less like you. You share much in common. Like the state you live in. Wisconsin.

It is night.

Of course, it's night. You are dreaming. Though there is nothing wrong with dreaming during the day. I did some of my best dreaming in sunlight. Once upon a time.

Open your eyes. If you haven't already.

My name is Robert. My friends called me Bob. I'm going to ask your name, but don't say it out loud. I'll hear it if you just think it. That's the way it works with dreams. Let's try it.

What

is

your

name?

> *Bob puts his fingers to his lips to remind the audience not to answer out loud.*

Nice to meet you. Let's get started.

> *A stool appears. Bob sits. Nature sounds cease.*

As a boy, I was bullied because I was ... different. That's how it's always been. Perhaps you know what I'm talking about. I'm not telling you this to gain your sympathy. Being bullied made me stronger. I had to become strong to survive. I'm not complaining.

I had some help. A man named William. He lived in the biggest house in town, a "mansion," some people called it. He owned ... well, it seemed like he owned everything in town. The big house on the big hill with the big orchard. The big car. The mercantile store. Don't worry if you don't know what a mercantile store is. Every town had one, and it was important. He also owned the zinc works. At least one member of every family in our town—and in towns miles around—worked at the zinc works. Or they worked the mines that provided the ore for the zinc works. William profited from all of it.

Then the mines petered out. There might have been enough ore left in the ground to open new mines, but the market for zinc tanked, just like the market for lead half a century before. The mines closed. The zinc works closed. The town emptied out.

By the time everything collapsed, old man Gundry had more than enough money, especially since he had no children of his own. He was the last Gundry in Mineral Point.

I always had this love/hate relationship with my hometown. It had a fairytale beauty that was pure magic, from its rolling hills and abundant trees, its star-filled skies and babbling streams, to its quaint stone cottages and storefronts.

But the people—the people were mean to me. Except for William. He saw what I was going through and he understood it. When I was grown, he encouraged me to leave and even helped me do it.

I tried London, but it didn't suit me. There I discovered a different kind of meanness, one that looked down on country boys from America's Midwest. William was disappointed when I showed back up in Mineral Point. He urged me to return to London. And I almost did. Until I saw the wrecking balls.

They were tearing down the old stone houses, one by one. The only good thing about this miserable town, in my personal experience, had been these magical abodes. Empty and abandoned now, one by one they were being destroyed. And for a moment, I imagined myself a character in a storybook, standing in front of the wrecking balls, saving the magic.

I could never do it, not alone. I had the courage, perhaps, but I didn't have the skills.

That's when I met Edgar. My Edgar. He was even more timid than I. But gesture by gesture, word by word, sentence by sentence, I drew him out. Embrace upon embrace.

Edgar had skills. We restored one cottage. We opened our restaurant and our shop. We restored another cottage. And another. People came. Not people from Mineral Point. God no. Our customers came from Chicago, Madison and from far, far away.

William worried for our safety. I did, too. What we were doing was dangerous. But I knew what I wanted.

We were two men in the 1930s and '40s, living together, fixing up old cottages, running a modest restaurant and, oh yes, an antique shop. We hid in plain sight. We didn't fool anyone, but so long as no one talked about what we were doing behind closed doors, and so long as those doors remained firmly closed, the townsfolk let us live our lives. After all, we brought visitors to this bankrupt town. And visitors spent money.

Over time, we saved more houses—even William Gundry's mansion. I'll never forget that day. The wrecking crane cast a dark shadow over the manicured grounds. It had already destroyed one of the outbuildings. I invited everyone I knew—and a lot of people I didn't—to show up that morning. Edgar told me what to say, and magically it worked. I passed around our favorite china teapot, and when we were done, there was just enough money to buy out the wrecking contract. Orchard Lawn, it's called today, and you can visit it. It's beautiful.

You can visit where Edgar and I lived, too. It's called Pendarvis. Edgar chose the name, borrowed from a small Cornish fishing village. The state owns Pendarvis now, which means—*you* own it.

What is it they say? If a butterfly flaps its wings ...

Toward the end of our lives Edgar and I couldn't live together. I hated that. We grew too old to keep running the business, and without the business, there was no handy excuse to explain two men sharing a house with one bed. But then, when I was dying, Edgar took me in. My last days were as they should have been.

I hear your thoughts. You are worried. A wrecking ball darkens the future of this great state and nation. You've seen more than enough evidence of its power of destruction. You fear for your children's dreams.

But look at it from my point of view:

If Edgar and I had ever been caught simply holding hands, it would have been the end for us. That's the Wisconsin where I lived my entire life. We were never once allowed to publicly acknowledge our commitment to each other.

Today I can stand on this stage in front of you and tell you that I loved Edgar Hellum and he loved me. If he were alive today, I could get down on my knees and ask him to marry me. He'd probably still be cautious. But eventually he would say yes. And we would have the most magnificent wedding ceremony ever. We'd hold it at Orchard Lawn. We'd serve Cornish pasties. And you would all be invited.

And Mineral Point? No longer a ghost town. Almost the whole town is on the National Historic Registry, and it's filled with farmers and artists and shopkeepers and chefs, working and living in old stone houses and storefronts. And on certain days of the summer, the streets are filled with rainbow flags.

I never, in my wildest imagination, pictured such a thing possible. That's how much better things are now, for people like Edgar and me. For all of us, really. For you.

Close your eyes.

Nature sounds resume.

This dream is almost over.

Close your eyes.

And when you open them ...

Things will be better for you, too.

And for your children.

That's the way it has to be.

That's the way it will be.

Butterfly wings.

END

The Power of Place

Jerry Apps

Mention the word *place*, and everyone knows what that means, or they think they do anyway. It means a notation on a map; Mineral Point is a place, and so is the Driftless region a place. But this is merely one definition of place. Place is much more than a location on a map. The place where we grew up has a major influence in determining who we are as people. Thus, place has power. As we grow older and move away from home, the physical place where we were in childhood continues to influence who we are. Secondly, finding out about a place involves more than accumulating the facts about it. Truly knowing a place involves the stories that can be told about the history of the place.

"The notion of the power of place suggests that place somehow has the potential to influence behavior, attitudes, and beliefs." Winifred Gallagher has explored this idea, highlighting its significance, making the concept of place a powerful component of our society.

Winifred Gallagher stated in her book *The Power of Place: How Our Surroundings Share Our Thoughts, Emotions, and Actions*: "Geography is more than the terrain and physical makeup of the world. It is the culture, education, conditions, foods, politics, language, and opportunities. These things make people and places unique, and capture the true meaning of Human Geography." (Gallagher, 2007).

I often told my college students that who they are is largely influenced by where they have been, by the places where they have lived. Many of the values and beliefs we have today have been influenced by places. Place is a powerful teacher. Its teachings are often hidden, but we are learning nonetheless.

As an example, I was born and raised on a farm during the Great Depression. We had no electricity until I was in high school, no indoor plumbing as long as I lived at home, no central heating. We heated our drafty farm home with two wood stoves—one also served as a cook stove. From the time we were little kids, my two brothers and I had chores to do every day. No complaining. As we got older, we graduated to higher-level chores, like helping milk the cows. We milked them by hand for many years.

I walked a mile to a one-room country school with all eight grades, where one teacher taught us. The school had no electricity when I began first grade, and it never had indoor plumbing. I learned the importance of helping other students with their lessons as they helped me. I learned how to share my lunch with kids much poorer than me. It wasn't something special to do; we just did it because it seemed like the right thing to do.

Our farming community consisted of several ethnic groups: German, Norwegian, Welsh, Polish, Russian, English, and Bohemian. They were our neighbors. They helped us, and we helped them. We got along with them, even though several knew little English and had habits and work approaches different from ours. They made up our community. They belonged to our place in the Chain O'Lake School District in Waushara County, Wisconsin. Our place was so much more than a spot on a map. I and the other kids who grew up there learned about life and living, work and play, loving and appreciating what we had, without knowing we were learning these things.

Whether we are aware of it or not, we each bring with us this early learning that was an important part of our childhoods. These learnings continue to influence us today. They are a foundation for what we do, when we do it, and how we do it. As we go through life, we bring this foundation with us, and if we are thoughtful about it, we examine these beliefs and values and decide which ones are worthy to carry forward and which should be left behind.

I still have the important beliefs and values with me and continue to follow the value of work, helping others when they need help, respecting and caring for the land, being on time—my dad said if you arrived fifteen minutes before an appointment, you were late—and getting along with others even though they may be different from me.

I express who I am, where I have been, and what I value through stories. I have never forgotten my dad's advice to never forget to look in shadows and listen to the whispers, meaning look where others may not choose to look, and listen to those who may choose to speak quietly and resist shouting.

As I confront new situations and arrive in new places, I have learned the difference between gaining information about that place and knowing it. Knowing is considerably deeper than simply being informed. Knowing involves the heart as well as the mind. Knowing involves emotions.

Here is an example of how I have come to know a place different from where I grew up. In 1966 my family bought a one-hundred-acre farm two miles from the home farm. We were living in Madison at the time.

During my growing-up years, I gained considerable information about this farm, its owners, and its successes and failures. When the farmhouse burned, the mother and son who lived there moved away, and the farm lay vacant.

After we bought the place, my wife and I did a quick inspection. We walked around the place, discovered the steep hills and valleys, discovered rocks, big and little, and stopped by the beautiful little pond in one of the valleys. It was highly questionable as a commercial farm, meaning someone making a living farming on this land. I had known this by watching the previous owners, who were too poor to have electricity and heated their tired old farmhouse with a wood stove, farmed with horses, and didn't even own a car.

The farm suited my family's purposes perfectly. Ruth and I saw this old, worn-out farm—as some of the neighbors described it—as a retreat away from the hustle, bustle, and noise of the city. I wanted a place where I could introduce my kids to nature and the outdoors that was more than a city park. We had three little toddlers at the time. And I wanted a place to relax, write, and enjoy the quiet.

But something was missing. I had a fair amount of information about the place, but I didn't "know" it. Some years earlier, my dad, among his other teaching, helped me learn the difference between being informed and knowing something. He suggested both were important, but being informed of a place was only the beginning. There was much more to a place than information about it.

I began the process of "knowing" my farm, which we call Roshara. I began by examining the land formation, the reason for the steep hills and deep valleys, and the stones—some mere pebbles, some as large as a small automobile. I learned that my farm was on the terminal moraine by digging through books, reports, and internet searches. Our land was part of the Green Bay Lobe, where one of the last glaciers that visited Wisconsin had retreated some ten thousand years ago. I have huge boulders that the glacier brought to our farm from Canada and left here.

I learned about the Native Americans who arrived

here shortly after the glacier receded and lived off the land. Wisconsin became a state in 1848, and before and after that, many treaties were signed with the Native Americans, taking the land from them and making it available for sale to white settlers.

Emma and her son, Weston Coombes, owned the farm before we bought it. I had known the Coombes family since I was a kid, as Weston Coombes had often worked for my dad on our home farm about two miles south of where I'd grown up. I had talked with Emma Coombes several times when I was a teenager. She told me about the Menominee Indians, who had lived on this land before several treaties were signed. Even after the treaties, which allowed the sale of the land to white settlers, a group of Menomonie Indians walked across what is now our farm from their trapping and maple sugar grounds in what is now Adams County. They traveled to Berlin on the Fox River, where they would trade their maple syrup and furs for other supplies. They would stop at what is now our farm and camp by our pond.

Emma was the daughter of the land's first white settler, Tom Stewart. She told me stories of how the Menominee often stopped by their farmhouse and traded maple syrup for salt. I found the first survey map of the Town of Rose (1851), which shows the Indian trails cutting across the township, across our farm.

One day when Emma was telling me these Native American stories, she brought a pail in from the porch and showed it to me. It was nearly filled with Indian arrowheads that her son had plowed up when he cultivated the land near our pond, the site of their temporary camps.

With Emma Coombes' stories, and my research, I began to know our farm. The more I dug out its stories, its history, the more interesting the place became. Next

I dug into Emma Stewart's father's history. He originally came from Rose, New York. He served in the Civil War and homesteaded our farm in 1867. I eventually wrote a book about the history of our farm in my quest to come to know this place, not merely be informed about it. (*Old Farm: A History,* Wisconsin Historical Society Press, 2013.)

One important dimension of getting to know a place—to understand its power—is to know its stories. When you come to a place, you may note its population, learn something about the people who live there, what they do for a living, what they do for fun, and where they came from. This is a good beginning, but you should ask the residents: What are the place's stories, and where do I find them? Also, let's not forget that every old building has a story to tell. Every piece of land has a story to tell, every hill, valley, village, city, river, and stream. All have stories waiting to be told. Coming to know a place is often buried in its stories.

The power of place resides in the heads of the people who have worked to understand the place and to know it. There is great power in knowing—especially about a place.

Sea Wall

Denise Thornton

The team we gathered to build our timber frame house was a group of artists, working in construction as their day jobs, and when it came to setting our stone foundation, they all agreed Tom should take the lead. A lanky guy with a graying ponytail, Tom carried a dog-eared copy of *Living the Good Life* with him everywhere. Helen and Scott Nearing's self-published 1954 chronicle of their move to rural Maine has been the bedrock for many a back-to-the-land journey, and includes a how-to guide for building a strong, straight stone wall.

Doug and I were feeling our way toward building the greenest house we could—both a home and a laboratory of sustainable shelter ideas with a carbon footprint the size of a baby's bootie. That meant passive solar design and locally sourced, natural materials like the generations-old limestone foundations of the faded red barns along our country road.

Thirty years earlier, during Doug's postdoc in the Netherlands, we found ourselves renting a three-hundred-year-old farmer's cottage along the edge of what was originally a Roman road. It stretched our sense of what a house could be to include axe-hewn timbers supporting wattle and daub walls and a thatched roof. We ate our *boerenkool* (a Dutch staple of potatoes and kale), tucked our daughter into bed, and dreamed through the long winter nights in a structure that has sheltered families for centuries. So when it came to constructing our own house, no envelope-pushing idea seemed like a bridge too far. We were determined to lay a foundation for our home that might last as long as that Dutch cottage.

The land the Nearings returned to was rich in a hard,

igneous rock created four hundred million years ago when magma cooled and solidified deep underground. Our Wisconsin rock is somewhat softer—soft being a relative term if you drop a chunk on your foot. Our bedrock was formed about five hundred million years ago when Wisconsin lay near the equator beneath a warm, shallow sea teeming with creatures whose shells drifted to the ocean floor, bonding with quartz sand and compressed over eons.

We paid a visit to Swiggum Quarry about ten miles away. Some of their limestone was broken into pieces of about the right size, and they glowed a pleasing, yellowish tan on that sunny morning.

I jumped on board when I realized this kind of rock could be chock-full of fossils, especially trilobites, that flourished into thousands of shapes and sizes from three inches to three feet in that ancient sea. Primeval precursors of insects and crustaceans with a pleasing pattern of triple ridges down their backs, trilobites grew by molting—each little fellow trailing a series of exquisite exoskeletons in its wake.

Wisconsin's state fossil, the *Calymene celebra*, was an adorable little trilobite scavenger who could have fit into the palm of your hand. Were they around today, you might keep one scuttling across the bottom of your aquarium. Good luck catching him before he burrowed under the sand!

Peter Brannen, in *The Ends of the World*, dubbed trilobites the standard bearer for the Paleozoic Era. They survived the End-Ordovician mass extinction 444 million years ago and the Late Devonian 360 million years ago, but burrowing could not save them from the End-Permian mass extinction about 250 million years ago, called the Great Dying, when 96 percent of all species then alive were wiped out of existence. Intense volcanic activity in Siberia threw sulfur and CO_2 into the atmosphere, causing brutal global warming and acid rain.

Trilobites that had scurried across the sea floor for three hundred million years were suddenly slime, along with almost every creature in the oceans, as well as those who had crawled onto land and evolved into reptiles—some as big as the dump truck that delivered our stone. By the end of the Permian, large and small, nearly all of them had perished.

The world in which trilobites thrived is long gone, but their fossils jut out of the rock around here in places where roadbeds have been cut through the hills. Some of our state's richest roadside fossil viewing is just minutes away from our land. We'd ordered a truck full of rocks and received a treasure trove of relics in the bargain.

Tom was not best pleased with the quality of our rock when he saw the pile next to our house site. We belatedly learned that the rock from Swiggum Quarry is not generally considered attractive enough for building or landscaping and is usually crushed for roadbeds.

Okay. So our stone was not ideal, but when you're building a house with a sod roof, you are already (apologies to R. Frost) far down a path, off the path less traveled by. We forged ahead, helping Tom set up plywood forms and began to set stone knee walls that were basically straight and definitely strong.

Each stone was contemplated, then pivoted to fit its flattest side against the frame more or less snugly next to its siblings. We shoveled concrete in to fill the gaps and let it set up before pulling away the wooden forms and moving them on to shape the next section of wall. Because our stone was not as flat and smooth as Tom would have wished, concrete often oozed and hardened between the rock faces and the plywood. Every day of fitting stone was, therefore, followed by two days of chipping concrete off the rock fronts. The perfect tool for this dirty job turned out to be some of the smaller chunks from our rock pile.

Squatting in front of our growing wall, pounding away errant concrete globs, I felt as close as I've ever been to prehistoric humans who hollowed out canoes and shaped their own shelters with a rock in hand, though honestly, for someone with a cell phone in her hip pocket, it got a bit tedious. Bang upon endless bang. Each impact transferred through the bones in my hand and resonated up my arm. An hour of chipping felt like an epoch, but the wall slowly took shape, and the rock pile shrank.

We had almost enough rocks for the job, but Tom and I eventually had to take his rusty pickup back to the quarry to find the best stones we could for the final push. Rick, the quarryman on duty, weighed our empty truck at the entrance and warned us to work fast because they were setting up to blast deeper into the rock face that day.

We wound our way through the lifeless, lunar landscape until we found a pile that looked promising and were picking through it for useable chunks when Rick roared up in a gigantic dump truck. Time to get out of the quarry. Now!

Dropping the rocks we were holding, we hopped into Tom's truck and raced after him to where Jerry, one of the explosives technicians, was waiting at the entrance. He phoned his partner. Three warning honks reverberated, then a crack like doom shook the valley.

Jerry told me he blows something up just about every day. Swiggum Quarry, he said, gets "shot" about twice a year. He grinned when I asked him if his partner had plunged a handle to detonate that mayhem. Explosions these days, I learned, were triggered by a handheld device with two yellow buttons and a red light.

No sticks of TNT either. Acetic acid, the main ingredient in his explosives, was transported by tanker truck. Jerry and his partner always mixed the explosives on site to avoid driving around with a volatile load that could come to a bad end on a train track or in a highway pileup.

Before the dust had drifted away, Tom and I rushed straight for the new blast site. My nerves were still jingling from the explosion, but I was pumped at the prospect of fresh rock. Local and fresh? How good can roadbed rock get?

As we approached the avalanche, Tom looked at me with a raised eyebrow. We were both struck by a distinctly pungent smell. I stopped and closed my eyes. I knew that smell, though I had never before smelled it in Wisconsin. Could we be inhaling the long-trapped scent of an ancient ocean? I filled my lungs deeply and held it as long as I could.

That overpowering sense of sea breeze dissipated quickly as we loaded the truck, and soon we were sweating in the same hot, dusty air we had been breathing before the blast. We filled the pickup with enough rock to finish our foundation, got weighed again, paid twelve dollars, and left.

The next few days, as I mindfully fitted those rocks into the last of the wooden forms, I found myself inhaling hopefully as I hefted each stone, imagining that long-lost sea bottom beneath my feet.

Later that week I called up Richard Slaughter, the director of the University of Wisconsin–Madison Geology Museum, who maintained that I could not have been inhaling the odors of an ancient ocean. Though Paleozoic seas might well have smelled a bit like their modern counterparts, I was assured that any such smell in our limestone had been washed away by millions of years of fresh groundwater.

Still, ten years later, when I look at our sturdy, fossil-studded foundation, I believe that I did once inhale the last breeze of a lost world where trilobites scuttled freely across a warm and friendly ocean floor, as if they could go on forever.

48

SECTION TWO

Neighborhoods

Grant County

Jacquelyn Thomas

Beneath the heel pad of Wisconsin's open palm (kitty-corner its frostbitten thumb), the bluffs of Dubuque clasp the cuff of Illinois with a rail bridge that pivots like a toggle. This has nothing to do with us. The ships that slip through that Mississippi turnstile are too wide for our rivers or creeks, and our depots are all private residences now, or farm sheds and kiosk museums. It's Norwegian of me to begin by noting the industry of others.

I first learned of Janteloven (the law of Jante) when a marriage counselor asked which of my ancestors had emigrated from Norway. Why would he assume one had? I'm dark-haired and ruddy with nondescript cheekbones and rarely, if ever, drink coffee.

"You deflect your husband's compliments," he said, "and respond with self-denigration."

I considered this, though I'd never felt Norwegian, and determined he must be right: my humility was overly robust, my modesty far too showy. I should tone it down—to save my marriage and end this surly bickering.

It would be years before I puzzled out the spelling of *yantah-lohven* and read the unspoken code of conduct, but in a coincidence that felt like intention, I saw it enacted that night.

The Holiday Folk Fair was underway in Milwaukee, and Sherman Middle School was handing out tickets. Ask our children, or their neighborhood friends, and they'll remember my husband *pushing the whip* down I-95 to bypass that field trip bus. Everyone knew that car, a rusted gold beast whose passenger door screeched when the hand reaching through a cranked-down window lifted its latch from outside. *The hooptie*, neighbors called it, climbing inside it—and those who never needed or asked for a ride: *that hooptie*, they said, shaking their heads. When its muffler detached, with sparks and a hullabaloo of alarm, my husband stood with his hand held out, mine snaked inside my shirt, and he reattached our muffler with my bra.

The thin fabric glued to its ceiling had been droopy and loose for some time. In the wind of an open highway, it ballooned. Each time we pressed it back up, it stretched and fought back. Kids on the bus, spying us trawling beside them, shot single-fingered fists out open windows. Ours would have done the same but for the struggle of hand cranks and being battered by a shroud. Instead, a pantomime war broke out: kids pointing down at us, faux-thrashing hysteria, mine leaning back, hands behind their heads, play-acting luxury.

My husband took his sweet time before pressing his foot on the gas. He understood that waving demurely, as if atop a convertible or tissue paper float, meant my heart was airborne. If this were a movie, it would be silent as my farmgirl childhood, but with intertitle placards:

"Look at Us!"—stuntin' as if on the come up and altogether feelin' ourselves.

"Look at You!"—mean mugging us like we play too much.

And all of us clownin' all of us. *"Fuck Jante!"*

This was the culture I loved—bosses who owned rule eight—as those bus kids would, not twenty minutes later, flying by as we huddled at the shoulder watching my man wrestle lug nuts. Of course, it was jacked-up: that bald and lopsided tire, our electrified static cling hair, the stress of free tickets that might go to waste, our marriage. So we hollered back and knotted our fists, ever ready to laugh defiantly and with relief, as everyone did in the projects we called home for five and a half months and thirty-one years.

Janteloven has just ten rules, in keeping with the number of commandments appropriated from the Jews, not the ninety-five complaints one might expect of Lutherans. Here it is, from Wikipedia:

1. You're not to think you are anything special
2. You're not to think you are as good as we are
3. You're not to think you are smarter than we are
4. You're not to convince yourself that you are better than we are
5. You're not to think you know more than we do
6. You're not to think you are more important than we are
7. You're not to think you are good at anything
8. You're not to laugh at us
9. You're not to think anyone cares about you
10. You're not to think you can teach us anything

Essentially, this repetitive kettle of fish boils down to the scalding bare-bones grunts of a salty German father that were only sometimes echoed, bland as Norwegian seasoning, by my mother.

They didn't tell us *not* to do things but expected us to know when to knock it off or when we were gettin too big for our britches and askin' for a lickin'. Statements were met with silence or "quitcher bellyachin'." These were the universals. Our mom answered questions with questions. "Why?" "Why do you think?" Or riddles. Her favorite color was sky-blue-pink. Our dad only jerked up his chin, rolled his eyes into boiled eggs, and rumbled: "Git. Git git git." And so, I did.

At the folk fair we sat in bleachers and watched Polynesians dance—mesmerized to a stupor, levitating on lapping waves—then the Russians jutted in, bouncy blue threads of Greeks, crisp-legged Irish, feathered Kenyans. We held our breath, studying dances from

India, swayed when Mexican girls waved be-ribboned skirts, and whistled because we recognized the Hmong. It was brilliant—the cascade of colorful sound beneath a waltzing light, the skittering, stomping, and swirling kaleidoscope of feet—until the Norwegians wandered in to loosely form a square. The women had bibbed aprons over their long-sleeved dresses. Men wore slacks and suspenders. Everything was gray, except shirts and aprons, every stocking in heavy black shoes. The fiddling was soft but bright, as if jigging in a meadow, percussion the stomp and three taps of a stressed metronome. Sometimes the men took hold of their suspenders and shuffled from side to side. Sometimes the women fanned half their skirts and wobbled with a hand at the hip. I think there were muted hand-clapping games, men on one knee tethered to orbiting ladies, and partner spins with clasped hands, arms held behind backs—as if drearily skating on ice. *My people*, I thought, *are a monochrome: moving, but like a flipbook of pilgrims on quaaludes.*

At the food stalls we studied dumplings, empanadas, and wontons as if visiting a museum, then gave the children change for popcorn and root beer. What we wanted were souvenirs. I'm certain all three children chose something, though no one remembers what, and that my husband declined their kind suggestions by playfully feigning disdain. As for me, I came away with two things I have to this day. First, a pair of wooden shoes that perfectly fit my feet—practical, I told myself, cheap because they're unpainted but useful in the community garden, pointed at the toe for lifting fishing nets and probably muddy hoses, easier to put on than boots and solid enough for shoveling snow—an extravagance, but wasn't I supposed to be practicing a less modest life? The lucky seventh time I stopped by that stall, the

Dutchman cut the cost. By half. What I love most is the horse-hoof sound. Three decades later, I still feel like a badass on concrete.

The second thing was free: an impromptu demonstration of Janteloven.

I wasn't lying when I said I liked it, the banquet-hall-sized painting suspended behind her table. She blinked a bit. Turned to look over her shoulder. Caught me staring at her embroidered vest. "*Ja-dat,*" she said, waving off mountains, a valley, its river and lake of sky, the elegant deer sipping with heads between delicate knees, still in the shadow of evergreens. "Dat pitcher fell one time, and the Danes hadda help us. Dey got it up."

So what? How was this not a simple midwestern exchange? I would have dismissed it but for the burr in my head (deflection, denigration), that sharp grinding of gears swearing I was rude and genetically ruined. And what of their ratchet cousins: disparagement, deprecation, negation. Why would any culture append them to the self? Sure, she deflected my compliment and handed it to Denmark, but it's not like self-effacement leads to self-erasement. I wanted to laugh it off—my psychiatric diagnosis—as Norwegian, but I did wish she'd just said thank you.

At the time, I hadn't yet read the laws of Jante. They're harshest, as written by a tertiary crowd. Translated from the original by Eugene Gay-Tifft (1936), Janteloven is archaic English with clarifying italics. (The sidenotes are mine, for my hicks and homies.)

1. Thou shalt not believe thou *art* something. (Fitcher-britches. Don't front.)

2–7. Be loyal to the collective (Farm Co-op. Posse.) Thou shalt not believe thou art as good as *we*. Thou shalt not believe thou art more wise than *we*. Thou shalt not fancy thyself better than *we*. Thou shalt not believe thou knowest more than *we*. Thou shalt not believe thou art greater than *we*. Thou shalt not believe *thou* amountest to anything. (*We* have/got your back.)

8. Thou shalt not laugh at *us*. (Bullshit. Bullshit.)

9. Thou shalt not believe that anyone is concerned with *thee*. (*We* minds its business.)

10. Thou shalt not believe thou canst teach *us* anything. (*We* mind *our* business.)

Janteloven is not special. See: Tall Wheat (Greece). Tall Poppies (Rome). Tall Poppy Syndrome (New Zealand and Australia). The nail that sticks up gets hammered down (Japan). Pull the jacket (Chile). Don't put your head above ground level (Netherlands).

None of this is real. *En Flyktning Krysser Sitt Spor* (1933) is a work of fiction. Jante does not exist. If it did, it would be in Denmark. Aksel Sandemose, né Axel Nielsen, was a journalist and essayist, a sailor, a teacher, a lumberjack, and the author of a satirical novel. Granted, it has 3.61 stars on Goodreads, with 647 ratings and 56 reviews, but I wonder about any readership attracted by its Kirkus review: "A psychological study of a fantasy life, of morbidity, fears, perversions, love-hate motivation, abnormalities." Who wants to spend time inside that?

Of course, I have. I read everything, peeling pages as if curing scurvy by slurping words.

The only books we had on the farm were the *Collier's Encyclopedia* set and *Junior Classics* collection in a windowsill-high bookcase in the front room. I think of them as Mom's wooden shoes. She was sad the year we lived in the city when the first boys were one and two, and I was only three. Dad had a factory job making office supplies. After work, he had bowling buddies, card partners, and gas in the car. When a door-to-door salesman came to the door—free delivery, case included, choice of covers, monthly payments, practical for

55

children when they start school—she said yes to both sets, which qualified her for the bonus prize: a cardboard fireplace.

Every Christmas it was brought down from a crawl space upstairs, the box it came in a little more battered each year, while the half-life-sized fireplace remained, to my mind, pristine. She had to fit the dozens and dozens of little tabs into slots to shape those cartoonish red bricks with tools printed to one side, the black-matte mantle and white brick hearth, brown log on fire between andirons. She took such good care of all our fragile things but never opened those books. If he could, Dad would've burned them in those cardboard flames. Being lazy, he called it, whenever he found me with one on my lap, sitting around doing nothing. *Gawn-now*, I said in my head—*git*.

I first learned Dad might not be my father when Grant County finalized their divorce—the summer I turned forty-nine—months before what would have been their golden anniversary.

Jiggs, the landlord, sold the farm out from under him years and years before Mom kicked him out. By then, he'd amassed several junky rental houses in town—and a machine shop, where he slept in the rumble seat of a pink Model T restored for car shows and parades.

So I'm told. I've never seen it.

I wonder why Sandemose changed his name. His father was Jorgen Nielsen. Aksel was born in Denmark. Only his mother, Amalie Jacobsdatter, was Norwegian. The name he chose was taken from her birthplace— Sandermosen Station. It's closed now, but the depot is still there, a pale-yellow building that looks like a house. "A hub for cultural activities," Wikipedia says. "A sculpture park is situated next to the track."

Funny how, when a secret pops out, people recover

so quickly from the surprise they claim to have seen it all along. You look nothing like him, or your siblings, my husband and children said. I knew what they meant but hadn't heard it before. Maybe because I have blond and brown-haired brothers, brunette and red-headed sisters.

I didn't have Dad's down-turned eyes, but I didn't have Mom's hooded ones either. It's the nose they were talking about. Mom's falls flat with an overhang like a mushroom cap. I don't have that. But his nose—and all the other kids have it—is everything. I think the medical term is fleshy, which means large. Think: russet potato.

My nose is like no one else's because I changed it myself. For most of fourth grade I sat with an elbow on my desk pressing my nose against the heel of my hand. I wanted a ski slope nose like the girl in the next seat and was told it was possible by Amy March.

I don't know how things written in books enter us and become real, but they do. An entire industry has materialized in Norway. International business professionals attend seminars on how not to transgress the invented laws of an imaginary town. Ask Scandinavia or Finland. Everyone knows Janteloven is fictional, a satirical bastardization, but they claim it and live with it anyway. Never once, not ever, did I suspect my father was not my father.

Here in the heel pad of Wisconsin's open palm, we're named for what we lack. We don't miss it—scraps of someplace else, bulldozed in and abandoned as drift. Being unglaciated means we are where we are and what we've always been: an ocean swarming with trilobites, mountains worn down by rain, and deep-cut valleys between steep folds of earth. Did it seem to them then, breaking land above the Kickapoo, a welcome blue harbor—or green changeling fjord?

Off paper, I'm a Pivot—a turnstile, a code-switch, a toggle. He is the schoolgirl crush who gave her candy before moving away in the fourth grade, sent her sweet letters from the city, and returned for a classmate's wedding in his formal Navy whites, knowing, as my mother said, "some things of the ways of worlds."

I've always been Norwegian. But the bohemian in me teared up when I read, "His heart let him down, and broke all of our hearts in the process" in Dr. Gurman's obituary. He wasn't Nordic, but he knew what he was talking about, and if he understood me at all, he knew why I cherish his obituary. The details are so rambunctious—"his club members, the Aardvarks, Cape Cod, pens, the color purple, yoga, fumbling with his iPhone"—and its transgression of Janteloven so old-timey and sweet it reads like an 1800s archive: "His scholarly contributions to the fields of Family and Couples Therapy, achievements, and awards were so plentiful that it would be impossible to list even a fraction of them without buying out the entire newspaper." Of course, I laughed. The deeper in the cut and from the gut, the more I love you.

Sometimes I'll say something so mean about myself, the only proper response is to break and double-up: "Ooh, snap!" My husband calls this a self-snap, and when he does, it never hurts.

"That's because you married a man who talks," my mother has said any number of times.

Word. Or maybe I taught him, and he let me because he doesn't practice the tenth law of Jante.

Timing matters. But it's more about place. My life splits evenly into two: a steep fold of earth above Pigeon Creek where the world was mostly sky, and the brick archipelago between railroad tracks near Oscar Mayer. Home is now a yellow-gold house equidistant to both, give or take two miles—the first and only place of our own—a giddy 401k hustle we unlocked a week before our opal anniversary.

Inside it, I unpack sound. A mandolin hangs on the guest room wall above a steel drum. Atop the armoire: a fat gourd shaker, djembe and güiro. My guitar stands in the closet beside a silver xylophone with parade harness and a bag of tambourines. Each reminds me of neighbors who jumped out of their skin when angry and were dry or dusty when bored. Acting scary meant you were the one afraid, and tripping had as much to do with drugs as dope. A woman I didn't know on the northside email chain sent URGENT SCREAMING messages no one could decipher and then apologized for any CONFUSEMENT—I read them for the endearing satisfaction of a single word. I loved the way rich folks became reach fucks in Spanish mouths, the Igbo neighbors who said *no toe-mah-toe-oh* when I offered them produce from the garden, how drinking gave Thais head eggs, and my archenemy blurted a word that budged my heart.

I suppose we had been telling her about herself, though no one called her out by name. We had valid complaints about the property manager, but her bossman was sitting right there, and we came overprepared. "How do you feel about that?" he asked.

She was clearly up in her feelings, and while I wasn't happy about that, I was also mad. She fidgeted in her chair and cut her eyes at everything but us. Sputtering a pen against her notebook, she spat: "Belliterate. I feel belitterate."

The collision of so many words at once: belittled, belligerent, illiterate, obliterate—the bass drum B and litter of t's, sad whine of ee's between feel and be—they gutted me, opening space to laugh. Not then, but later, and warmly. When my thoughts run bitter over her,

I reach for that word like a sugar-rimmed chaser. And though we never became friends, I embrace her.

This is why I call double bullshit on law eight. Thou shall not laugh at *us*. Shifting the italics from *us* to *at* changes nothing. Reflexively, I tried it myself. Not laughing is still the point. Modify this rule of Jante any way you want—swap out its governing preposition, let the subject and direct object trade places, remove the self-negating modal verbs—and it remains a sentence of silence. Humans are pattern-seeking animals on the hunt for sound. Words lead us, and stories feed us, but laughter is the fire we gather around.

Inheritance

Lynda Schaller

Those early Europeans swashbuckled through
this world they christened *New*, pushed
to all corners as if they owned the place.
And pretty soon they did.

My white settler ancestors did not wage
the conquest, did not draft
the writs of deceit,
        exile,
        control.

Nonetheless—my kin
staked futures on boundaried measures of earth,
swatches dissected from Ho-chunk country.
Did my forebears ever consider
the Indigenous inhabitants who belonged to this land?
Did they wonder who had once peopled their farms?
Or ask: How do they fare *now*—Where *are* they—

For those of us still occupying ill-gotten land:
it's a long learning curve toward humility.
When willing, we face seeming impossibility—
squaring up ancestral trespass, reckoning
unsettled debt, untangling entitlements.

This is hard, troubling work.
We risk shame, we hazard regret.

I am tempted to wrestle
this disturbing history

into tidy   comfortable   resolution.

I resist.
All I know now

        is to listen.

In The End

Steve Alden Nelson

The doctor says that this time, the release will not be a discharge, but rather a death certificate. The disease that has taken half of his stomach and one of his lungs has finally infiltrated the entire broken-down muscle and bone machine. Pointless to speculate on the cause, a single culprit, or a toxic cocktail of liquor and cigarettes along with the spraying of poison on other people's crops to increase the yield, inhaling fiberglass dust at a forty-hour-a-week factory, all of these tossed in with the ghastly nightmare of World War II, storming the midnight beaches of Normandy, heading full tilt and blind into the bloodshed with only a black and white photograph of his darling girl over his heart as armor.

The doctor says that you should get his affairs in order, a seemingly insurmountable task, trying to make order out of decades of chaos.

All eleven of your brothers and sisters will have their time alone with him, and now it is yours. You sit at the bedside of your father, tattoos from cancer treatments mapped across his used-up flesh. Knowing that at any moment he will be taking his final step off this macabre and shadowy carnival ride, what do you say to this man, seven years sober, when his last request is for a sip of whiskey? Your first instinct is to bolt to the nearest liquor store, return to his bedside, dip a finger in the amber liquid, and dab it on his parched lips, his soon-to-be forever silent tongue, letting him drift back to the days before it all got out of hand, before breeding twelve hungry children, when he could dance the night away with the prettiest girl in the county. You want to comfort him with Jim Beam the way that you would lay an orange blossom near the beak of a dying bird, but some of your

62

Christian siblings protest, insisting that he check out clean, as though the Lord will credit him for a handful of useless sobriety tokens and a dog-eared philosophy of one day at a time. And you want to tell them that it's too fucking late, that he's used up all of his miracles and won't live long enough to pay back the ones he borrowed or stumbled upon. But you don't, and you let him go without. And before the sun sets on that mid-October afternoon, he is gone.

The following summer, you're in Minneapolis at an outdoor concert in Loring Park, drinking cold beer on a scorching hot afternoon in mid-July. These are the days before smartphones. So, you are blissfully unreachable, mingling with strangers. Suddenly, and quite literally, out of the clear blue sky, a black cloud crawls up the backside of the old Guthrie Theater, and within minutes, you're soaked to the skin and sent racing back to your apartment, dancing in newborn mud puddles, during which time, one hundred twenty miles south, paramedics are loading your mother into an ambulance, transporting her broken heart to the nearest medical facility, thirty miles away, through slow, snaking hairpin turns, across endless stretches of exhausted asphalt, and across the mighty Mississippi, wider now than any ocean. It has been exactly nine months since your father passed away, and several days later, you bury your mother next to him near the edge of a cornfield on the outskirts of the small midwestern town where you'd all grown up. After the service, you return with your eleven siblings to the modest, wood-framed house at 505 North Kingston Street that will, from now on, never again be called home.

You remain on the front porch while the rest of the family goes in to begin dividing up your parents' few belongings. And you say to yourself, "I don't want the television set or the washer/dryer. Don't give me the refrigerator or the run-down Pontiac in the dirt driveway. Don't give me pots and pans, dishes or knives. Don't give me empty condolences or heavenly reasons why I am now an orphan.

"Give me my father's worn-out work boots, two sizes too big. I'll wear extra socks. Give me the imitation crystal rosary that my mother kept beneath her pillow, the beads worn down from a billion Our fathers and Hail Marys offered up to a mostly non-responsive god."

Then it occurs to you that you'll never again climb the crooked steps to the second-story bedrooms where window panes were once jammed partially open, and wads of newspaper filled the cracks in the glass. You will never sleep there again on mattresses laid over wood plank floors, mismatched bedding, pillows stained by years of drool from too many children gone to bed hungry, salivating through nocturnal limbo.

You will never dream there again, dream on the front porch during warm summer mornings of a world too good to be true. You will drive by there again someday on your way to your sister's house down the block, but you will never knock on the front door and tell the current owners that despite all odds, magic came from that place. But you will write about it, and they may stumble across your words and recognize their own address.

"This is Your Pasty":
Queer Domesticity in the Wisconsin Driftless[1]
Christopher Hommerding

Shoulder steak, onions, potatoes, kidney suet, salt and pepper—this collection of simple ingredients, wrapped in a basic pie crust, composed a dish that during the 1950s and 1960s became the widely renowned Cornish pasty of the Pendarvis House restaurant in Mineral Point, Wisconsin. The Cornish dinners served at the small lead miner's cottage built in the 1840s garnered rave reviews by well-known American food critics such as Clementine Paddleford and Duncan Hines. The tiny restaurant tucked into the rolling hills of rural southwestern Wisconsin also appeared in the pages of publications like *Gourmet* magazine and was listed as one of the top seven restaurants in the nation by the *Saturday Evening Post*.[2] It was also owned and operated by two queer men, Robert Neal and Edgar Hellum.

Despite the restaurant's out-of-the-way location, the glowing recommendations of Pendarvis House did not go unheeded, as scores of diners flocked from all over Wisconsin and beyond to eat pasty in the one-room cottage and tour the ever-growing complex of historic buildings Neal and Hellum began to purchase and restore in the 1930s. But why all of this attention for a meal

---

1. Originally published as "This is Your Pasty: The Performance of Queer Domesticity in Small-Town Wisconsin," *Notches: (Re)Marks on the History of Sexuality*, October 8, 2015, https://notchesblog.com/2015/10/08/this-is-your-pasty-the-performance-of-queer-domesticity-in-small-town-wisconsin/.

2. Will Fellows, *A Passion to Preserve: Gay Men as Keepers of Culture* (University of Wisconsin Press, 2004); Mark H. Knipping and Korinne K. Oberle, *On the Shake Rag: Mineral Point's Pendarvis House, 1935–1970* (State Historical Society of Wisconsin, 1990), 28–29.

that was, as the proprietors themselves often admitted, essentially "peasant food"?[3] Much of the answer lies not in the food itself but in the men and the performance they provided. In their tiny stone cottage, Neal and Hellum curated and leveraged a particular vision of the Cornish history of their small town. The result was a queer domestic performance that elevated the simple pasty to a luxurious, gourmet meal, enveloping diners in an experience at once historic, exotic, and alluring.

In his study of the domestic lives of twentieth-century queer men in London, historian Matt Cook describes domesticity as "that elusive quality that made a 'house' a 'home.' It suggested clearly defined gender roles, and emotional, relationship and sexual lives enclosed within four walls."[4] To queer domesticity, then, according to historian Nayan Shah, is to upset "the strict gender roles, the firm divisions between public and private, and the implicit presumptions of self-sufficient economics and intimacy in the respectable domestic household."[5] Such was the case with Neal and Hellum. Their home, and in many ways their lives, were open to the public. The private space of their home became the public space of a restaurant, and their partnership—both in business and in life—was on clear display. Moreover, the entire operation was predicated on an inversion of gender roles, an inversion that saw two men taking on the role of housewives. This sort of gender inversion had long been understood as a marker of homosexuality and in other contexts drew theatergoers, film audiences, and tourists, who sought thrills outside the sanctioned

---

3. Edgar Hellum, interview by Will Fellows, December 17, 1997.

4. Matt Cook, *Queer Domesticities: Homosexuality and Home Life in Twentieth-Century London* (Palgrave Macmillan, 2014), 9.

5. Nayan Shah, *Contagious Divides: Epidemics and Race in San Francisco's Chinatown* (University of California Press, 2001), 14.

bounds of normative society.[6] For Pendarvis guests, flaunting convention, if only for the duration of a meal, was as important as a well-made pasty. Indeed, at Pendarvis House, the two went hand in hand.

Importantly, in their restaurant, Neal and Hellum were not performing the role of just any housewife, but their particular version of the Cornish housewife. In the 1820s, over a century before the restaurant became a tourist attraction, Mineral Point was a predominately male lead-mining outpost. A decade later, the town was a permanent settlement as entire families began moving to the region. This particular migration included a large influx of Cornish immigrants who brought to the area their knowledge of hard-rock mining. While the men brought their mining skills, Cornish women, according to Neal and Hellum's self-consciously narrated history, brought domestic stability to the region, a stability that included the pasty and the intriguing practice of the shake rag.[7]

Neal and Hellum explained to their guests that when Cornish women had finished preparing the noon-day meal, the housewives would stand outside their cottages and wave handkerchiefs in the air to signal to the men working the mines on the hill opposite that dinner was ready. This strictly gendered domestic practice gave rise to the name Shake Rag, a practice that Neal and Hellum adopted for both their restaurant and their preservation project. They even went so far as to request the city change the name of the street that ran in front of

---

6. George Chauncey, *Gay New York: Gender, Urban Culture, and the Making of the Gay Male World, 1890–1940* (Basic Books, 1994).

7. Marie G. Dieter, *The Story of Mineral Point, 1827–1941 (Writers Program of the Works Progress Administration, 1941*; repr. Mineral Point Historical Society, 1979); George Fiedler, *Mineral Point: A History* (State Historical Society of Wisconsin, 1973).

Pendarvis House to Shake Rag Street, a request that was granted in 1949 and followed by a state historical marker two years later.[8]

Neal and Hellum's story of the Shake Rag, however, was false. But its continued use spotlights how the partners self-consciously crafted and marketed a domestic past that they queerly reenacted—through gender inversion—for visitors. In 1953, the partners received a letter from the National Trust for Historic Preservation explaining that the name Shake Rag did not reference women shaking rags after their husbands and sons, but was instead "a mocking nickname, implying hunger or beggarliness."[9] Indeed, "Shake Rag" marked this part of Mineral Point as run-down, shoddy, and impoverished. Such connotations, however, do not sell pasties. In contrast, a portrayal of an idealized domesticity, however queerly rendered, proved profitable. As Hellum put it, dinners at Pendarvis House were a show and the restaurant "like a theater. We set the stage, you see."[10] Visitors received personal tours of the grounds and buildings stockpiled with luxurious antiques a nineteenth-century Cornish immigrant mining family could only have dreamed of. And all were party to a well-rehearsed meal. The star of the show—the pasty—took center stage at the very beginning of the meal (along with relish and pickle trays). At the appointed time, Neal would enter the dining room with the family-sized pasty on a large serving platter. "This is your pasty," he would say. "It was made especially for your party." The

---

8. Robert Neal, interview with William Scheick, 1954, Robert Neal Papers, Mineral Point Public Library; "Proceedings of the Regular Meeting of the Mineral Point City Council," *Mineral Point Democrat-Tribune*, May 12, 1949.

9. Helen Duprey Bullock to Robert Neal, January 12, 1953, Robert Neal Papers, Mineral Point Public Library.

10. Edgar Hellum, interview by Will Fellows, December 17, 1997.

supporting characters would follow: a second course of salad and crackers and a final dessert course usually featuring Cornish saffron cake, clotted cream, and fruit preserves. But not a Cornish housewife in sight.[11]

In the end, it mattered little whether or not the story of Shake Rag was true. And it mattered even less that the pasty was nothing more than a basic meat pie. Instead, what ultimately drew many visitors to Pendarvis was the queer domestic performance of Neal and Hellum. Consciously or not, these two men—one just a quarter Cornish, the other thoroughly Norwegian—capitalized on people's fascination with the curated and idealized past the partners reenacted. Here, in a small Wisconsin town, were two men living together, cooking, baking, decorating, serving food, selling antiques and in so doing, magically resuscitating homes otherwise doomed to be razed. The queerness of Neal, Hellum, and their business was there for all who chose to see it and all who chose to participate. One such visitor, a Madison newspaper columnist, asked of Neal, "Who are you? The Fairy Prince with the Magic Wand?" To which Neal replied, "No, I'm just Robert Neal of Mineral Point."[12] As it turns out, he and Hellum were both just regular guys and fairy princes, and their queer performance kept the magic of Pendarvis House alive for nearly forty years.

---

11. Mark H. Knipping and Korinne K. Oberle, *On the Shake Rag: Mineral Point's Pendarvis House, 1935–1970* (State Historical Society of Wisconsin, 1990), 28–29.

12. Betty Cass, "Madison Day by Day," *Wisconsin State Journal*, September 10, 1935.

Sun Settle Down, Shadow's Galore: A Love Letter to Nova

Jeremy Payne

Dear Nova,

As I sit down to write this love letter to you and our community, I am filled with a profound sense of gratitude and hope. Your mother and I moved to Mineral Point (MP) with big dreams and even bigger ambition in our hearts. It is here, in the rolling hills of southwest Wisconsin, right along the Pecatonica River, that we found a new home—a place where our family could breathe, experience, and just be. It has provided the fuel for the necessary collective care we extend to our surrounding communities. It is also the place where we conceived you, our miracle, after years of trying. The sincerity of Mineral Point, with its dynamic history and purported community, has become the backdrop to an era in our lives, shaping our experiences and our sense of connections to all living things in ecosystems.

In Mineral Point, we have found a unique blend of plight and politics, where artists and creatives live on Indigenous lands alongside generations of farmers, vibrant Latino communities, descendants of Cornish miners and Mennonite communities, diverse Black sacred siblings, and the people living in the "MP Driftless Shadows." It is a place of beautiful divergence, where the "Ole True Mineral Point Resident" and the persistent "New Mineral Point Resident" merge seamlessly, creating a tapestry of stories and lived experiences that are interwoven in truly interesting ways.

Our family has always been inspired by a common thread: the desire to extend happiness, safety, and ensure that everyone is well-resourced. As your parents, we are committed to teaching you the values of collective care, love, joy as resistance, and playfulness. We want you to grow up understanding the importance of true community defined by the collective, and to see beyond the dominant narratives that often overshadow the deep richness of the "shadows" of Mineral Point—the people and places that are often overlooked yet hold the truest wisdom and essence of this region. As they are often the first point of contact upon arrival.

The shadows of Mineral Point are where profound stories lie. These are the spaces and people who embody the collective spirit of the Driftless region—the sometimes disowned, the forgotten, the not from here, the odd, the weird, the perceived "trouble," the "sketchy," the exiled—personally, socially, economically, politically, insert another _____-ally. The Dollar General workers who stood up against what they described as "corporate greed" and walked out for fair wages and appreciation, the vibrant community at The Travelers Inn on Dodge Street and School House Apartments with their visible joy and hopes, and the elders at Mineral Point Health Services Nursing Home who bear the transferred exhaustion and harm of a broken healthcare system. The commendable 2024 Holiday Mutual Aid efforts to save local businesses and economic development to bring back important commerce to Mineral Point, yet the economically depleted individuals and families are left to pull themselves back up alone. Oh, the duality. All the while, Mineral Point is recognized by Travel Wisconsin's Top List, yet there is still so much more opportunity to extend the Mineral Point dream to so many more. These are the stories we want you to know, Nova, for they hold the lost wisdom of the Mineral Point Driftless Shadows.

Raising you in this area means truly leaning in and embracing the duality of our local experiences. As a Black father in Mineral Point, I have navigated the complexities of race, gender, and class, experiencing both joy and discrimination. It is a journey of constant refinement and adjustment, of processing and responding to internalized assumptions, and of finding harmony within the beautiful rolling hills and the fellowship of the community.

We want you to learn about the collective care that extends beyond our nuclear family, to understand the importance of group survival, communal living, and the dynamics of power and joy resistance. We want you to know the hopes, dreams, and fears of the people living in the shadows, and to recognize the beauty, resilience, and opportunities that exist within them.

Your mother and I are overly committed to nurturing your curiosity and ensuring that you grow up with a deep sense of critical empathy and understanding. We want you to explore the history of this region, as told from multiple perspectives, and to understand the significance of the Black miners who were once part of this community and Pleasant Ridge/Present-Day Beetown of Grant County, a short drive away, who demonstrated the truest possibilities of community and collective care. And to question why diverse Black representation in Mineral Point from 1990 to the present dwindled significantly. Explore the policies, practices, and norms. Hear the local stories and insights. We also want you to appreciate the contributions of the Latino migrant workers and the rich traditions of the Amish, Mennonite, and Indigenous communities.

Most importantly, we want you to know that you are part of a larger story—a story that is still being written.

Agency, opportunity, and responsibility. As we walk the rolling hills of Mineral Point, breathing in the fresh air and soaking in the beauty of the landscape, we are reminded of the importance of grounding ourselves in this present era while honoring the past. We are reminded that joy is a form of resistance and that it is essential for the maintenance of our body, mind, and spirit.

Nova, you are our miracle, and it is our honor to guide you through this journey. Together, we will continue to explore, learn, and grow, forging new connections with pockets and corners of community, always holding onto the values of love, joy, and collective care. This is our love letter to you and to the community that has embraced us.

I leave you with a poem I wrote shortly after your birth. We sat under a tree on a breezy Sunday. I rocked you in my arms, overwhelmed with emotions. Your beauty moved me. The Driftless landscape of Mineral Point also moved me. The leaves had fully turned color as fall was in full effect. Busting red and orange. You were just born.

Fall'n' Up

Restless and rupture.
Love is the Fall's bursting
plight, Beautiful wind, dry
happy tears.

With all my love, Dad

My grandmother was an unwanted child.
Hannah Adalance

Lady Liberty
took a bit of liberty
in saying
who deserved to get some.

America never wanted
my family.

When Grandmama was seven years old
she got on a giant boat
and floated 4,775 miles away from anything
she had ever known.

And thank fucking g-d
she did.

I once was in a room full of kids like me:
ancestors full of Jewish blood who crossed continents,

and every single one of them matched
so perfectly
to Jewish American history:

1800s pogroms in Russia,
the various waves of immigration
influenced by world events.

When it came time to me,
they said:
"Hannah—1930? That's impossible."

And it was.

In 1924, Congress passed a law that made it
practically impossible
for anyone not Western European "white"
to come to America.

And my grandmama was considered neither of these.
Definitions of "white" & "worthy" changing through the years.

How did my grandmama
sneak in
to America?

The mountains where she's from are in modern-day
    Ukraine,
its borders at the time shifting in each war.

When Grandmama set sail,
thousands of Jews called these Carpathian Mountains
home.

What does home mean
in the passage of time?
What does home mean
when there is nobody left alive?

What a happy dream
to imagine
that my grandmama's family
and relatives
were the lucky ones.

And wasn't she the luckiest?

My great-grandpa Avrum slid into Boston Harbor
nine months
before the Immigration Act of 1924.

And only because of *this*,
he could bring his wife
and children later,
when so many were denied.

America has such a strong history of denial,
of sweeping wretchedness
under the rug.

This act, the roaring twenties of America,
was to "preserve the ideal of U.S. homogeneity."

What a death sentence,
what a little law in a long history
of terrible ones.

The more I learn about America's immigration laws,
the more I realize that our present-day atrocities
are nothing new.

How good we all are
at not learning history
and letting it repeat.

My great-grandparents, my grandmother,
& her siblings
barely slipped in,
right under America's nose.

And all I can think about is
what if they didn't?
What if Great-Grandpa Avrum
had waited 'til spring?

My grandmother was twenty-one in 1944,
a young woman in America
(the Immigration Act still steel bars
around all edges of U.S. borders).

And back home, across the ocean and in the
    mountains,
the gradual bad got worse.

The ghettos that had been erected, the camps, the
death trains to Auschwitz that departed,
all the ordinary folks,
the ordinary families.

90,000 of the 100,000 Jews back in Grandmama's home
didn't make it.

90% who were not lucky
like my grandma.

You could say it started
many different times & ways,

White supremacy has such
an intricate history.

In 1941 was one start, when
18,000 Jews were deported from Carpathian Ruthenia
under the guise
of expelling Alien refugees.
How does all of this begin?
How does it end?

Who gets to flee violence
and poverty,
churning out bodies at home?

Who gets to bring their children?

Who is allowed to stay alive,
to pass down forgotten stories
in pieces of DNA?

Who does America decide
gets to be lucky?

America, *LADY LIBERTY*,
with one fist always
fighting for freedom, one hand
always locking the gate.

re LIGHT
Hannah Adalance

Today, the 15th of Kislev 5782,
I formally was embraced
and welcomed into the Jewish peoplehood.

I appeared before a Beit Din
and bared the vulnerability
of my desire to *belong*
to be wholly
unequivocally
Jewish:

no hyphens,
no qualifiers.

I cried when the Rabbis invited me back after
deliberations
and handed me
the certificate
formally welcoming
me.

Hannah Ruth
bat
Mordecai Shalom
v'Roxanne.

I sang Shema
in the Mikvah,
voice ringing
crisp
to G-d's ear,

the Universe
bending herself

into life
and blessings.

I emerged
(water dripping tiny Amens across
my wholly human experience).
I emerged,
a Jewish mujer.

I drove the many miles home
technology turning
vast spaces
into intimate moments.

I cried, looking at the hills
of the Driftless region,
drenched deeply in Autumn.

Belonging is not a winter coat
I've slipped on.

Belonging is the shiver
in my bones
put to rest.

Eternal light
warming
& flickering,
Ner Tamid

Oh, I will never be timid
only wrapped in awe,

my heart continuously rekindled
warming the sanctuary
of my body,
this ordinary life

to which I belong.

"Here-ness" in the Driftless

Justin O'Brien

My wife and I have lived in Mineral Point in the Driftless territory for nearly a decade, and yet I am still asked, "Are you from here?"

I have reacted at times to this question with near guilt, expressing my regret that I am not actually from here (and trying not to reveal too quickly that I moved here several years ago from a major city).

"No, we're not from here, but we live here. And we love it here," I have replied, as if that will assuage some of the stigma of shame from not having been born here.

The late, beloved stonemason, Rollie Sardeson, who was actually born and raised just a few miles from Mineral Point, is reported to have gruffly dismissed this pointedly probing question by saying, "I'm not from here ... but I got here as soon as I could."

It took me a while longer.

Many years ago, as a young couple with three boys, we began visiting Mineral Point, fulfilling a fascination engendered by a copy of *Mineral Point: A History*, given to my family by the author, native Pointer, George Fiedler, best man at my parents' wedding. From a shelf in our house I would take down his book to browse and to look at the illustrations of the old stone houses of Mineral Point rendered by local artist Max Fernekes. Then, in the 1980s, by grand coincidence, a good friend of ours moved to Mineral Point with his wife, and we began to visit them, driving the three and a half hours to spend long weekends here. We learned to love the area, its history, the people, and the unique geography of its driftless terrain.

I found myself drawn to the oak savannas, the distant mounds, the gentle hills and valleys of the Driftless territory carved eons ago by centuries of glacial melt from the icy north, the craggy outcroppings revealed from eroded soft layers of limestone, the contoured fields, and the stone homes, businesses, and farms of locally quarried rock. My city-driven blood pressure returned to normal levels when we'd come. And I felt strangely comfortable and familiar with my surroundings. I wondered what the Driftless may have awakened in me.

Carl Jung, wrote of the collective unconscious, the memories stored in our genetic history that contain deep "collective memories" of a people. My ancestors are Irish on both sides. Was I perhaps "remembering" a likeness to an ancient home of rocky fields, rolling hills, grand vistas, oak woods, country lanes—the landscape of my Irish predecessors?

Like the Cornish who came here to mine the lead ore, some of my Irish ancestors—Celtic cousins to the Cornish—were copper miners who came to work the mines of Michigan's Upper Peninsula, then eventually settled on the Iowa prairie. The tawny and rocky pastures, green fields, and wooded hills must have resonated deeply with the Cornish and the Irish, as these features resembled the wild, rocky, windswept headlands and farmlands at the very southwest tips of their respective countries.

The question "Are you from here?" may be an innocent one from a questioner who simply doesn't recognize the person. It may be small-town inquisitiveness: the questioner just wants to know the person. But it also may be a passive-aggressive means of probing a few details from someone viewed to be a "stranger"; the subject doesn't look like someone from here, is maybe too urban looking, or dressed differently, or has a perceivable accent, or a different skin shade.

But what is it, to be "from here" anyway?

In a small town such as Mineral Point, the questioner asking "Are you from here?" generally means not only were YOU born here, but were your parents born here, and were your grandparents born here? In this context, "here" implies a geographic birthright to a club that, in rural communities, is experiencing rapidly dwindling membership. If multi-generational residency is required to be from "here," there may soon be very few to claim "here-ness," and eventually, perhaps there may not even be the same "here" to be from. And it is worth noting that there once were many who pre-dated those asking, "Are you from here?" and who were most definitely from here and are no longer here. I am referring, of course, to the Native Americans who were from here—for centuries—until supplanted by white settlers, miners, and farmers.

Today, in order to grow, rural communities need to retain residents and attract additional ones. In order to thrive, communities need diversity—a diversity of skills, of age groups (namely families), and a willingness to be open to other aspects of diversity. Communities need residents who participate in the work of community and believe in the possibilities of community. Without this, there can be no community and no "here" to be from.

The question then ought to be re-framed from "Are you from here?" to "Do you believe in 'here,'?" "Do you wish to be part of 'here'?" And even more to the point, "Do you feel you belong?" here, in the endlessly possible Driftless.

Great-Grandpa O'Brien

Justin O'Brien

Our lanterns lit the stony path through the village
and up the steep, rocky hill, the ocean roaring at our
  backs,
and down we went into the mines—from dark to dark.
The black-edged hoe rusted in the thistle,
the needle lay idle in the longer pant leg,
time off only for the Lord.

Me and Tom Kelly lit out for England
and after our first ship wrecked off Wales,
refused passage on the coffin ship *Pomona*,
which then went down with 389 souls.
Spared twice, we made another way to Amerikay,
only to work in the Michigan mines
and it was dark to dark once more.

But I sent for Margaret and little Michaeleen,
and as I took copper ore from the rock
I set aside copper pennies from me pay
until there was enough for the farm,
and I traded breaking rock for breaking sod.
We had ten in all, and raised the lot
in the bright, expansive light of the Iowa prairie.

Wilma

George Hesselberg

When I took my little brother and our dog on walks around the block in the village of Bangor, we would stop and talk with Wilma, who would cheerfully indulge our interruption of her chores.

Wilma lived on the corner lot of the block next to ours. She drove an immaculate light brown Ford, late 1940s, early 1950s. The car was kept in a garage behind her house, facing the alley. It was my shortcut home when, years later, I worked late setting pins for a penny-a-frame at the Bangor Recreation Lanes, and it was my shortcut downtown on Saturday nights, so I have passed by Wilma's house and garage most of my life, and much of hers.

She worked for many years as Bangor's chief telephone operator, retiring when the village's party lines went dial in the early 1960s. Hers was the voice that said "Number please" in response to a whirl of the crank on the heavy, black telephone.

Wilma lived alone in a comfortable-looking, old white two-story house. It was nothing fancy—two steps up to the enclosed front porch entrance. There was a small porch over a root cellar at the back entrance.

Wilma's older sister needed care, so she came to live with Wilma in Bangor. The older sister had been there for several months, when one spring day, Wilma returned from an errand to find her sister had fallen down the narrow stairway to the basement.

How Wilma, 84, carried her sister, 87, back up those steps is a mystery.

But the sister was seriously injured in the fall, so she was sent to a nursing home. Wilma could no longer take care of her.

One sunny Saturday soon after this, I was home for the weekend to visit my parents when I took the alley shortcut downtown. It would have been remarkable to not stop to say hello to Wilma, who was filling her wash lines with whites, sheets, and pillowcases. I commented on the large laundry load, especially for a Saturday, but Wilma merely nodded and grabbed another pillowcase by its ear and silently attached it with a clothespin to the line.

On the Tuesday following, she was found dead in the small back porch to the home. Her checkbook was laid out on the dining room table, as were her two purses and a handwritten will. She had also purchased a wreath for her grave. She wrote that she was worried about her ill dog, Tiny. A note to her sister was on her pillow. Everything appeared to be in order.

I didn't hear if her laundry was clean and folded, but I'll bet it was.

Self-limiting
Andrea Larson

We are friends because
you live across the street
and you drink whiskey, like me.
Most of the time we laugh
at the same jokes
and we roll our eyes at the same
pretty girls.
We bake cakes to share
and then curse ourselves.
We pretend we are above
dreaming the same dreams.

We are friends because
you do not hear my call
and you're the type
to not call at all.

Self-Talk
Andrea Larson

Do not let yourself get precious
like some lost out-of-towner drawing her breath
at a charming vignette:
an old chair abandoned in a field.
It was made for a purpose and built to use.
We all are.

Do not let yourself get looked at like a pretty thing.

Hold your form, girl,
especially when the ones who swore to look after you
let you alone to rot.
The dead gave you no trash,
your muscle and bone tested and bruised,
worn smooth.
Say who you are:
a resting spot for the weary.

88

SECTION THREE
Flora & Fauna

to those everywhere else

Franciszka Voeltz

to those everywhere else
it's not that there is just *here* and *everywhere else,*
it's more complicated than that,
but here are the gifts
harvested from these ridges and valleys
to send to those
on the ocean coasts,
up in the mountain altitudes,
on the mesas and along the arroyos,
and where prairie once stretched
all along the flat forever—
small slices of here to carry with you:

1.

the clip-clop of the horse pulling a buggy
ahead of you along the two-lane highway,
how it forces a deceleration
until passing is safe
which often takes a while
on roads that curve as much as
these highways do—
shaped by the rises of ridges
and dips of valleys,
how some fight against the obstruction
and how some find gratitude
in the unexpected slowing down

2.

the clear cool creek rushing
a mile down the road from home,
a movement carried through each season
even on days when the outdoor thermometer
reads -18 degrees F

how, if you visit the water regularly,
the shape it takes and
the way it moves will tell you things
about the season you are in
one day it might bring you the high-pitched chitter
of an eagle landing on an outstretched pine branch
or the silence of a great blue heron
cruising warm currents overhead
only seen because you were looking—
your cheeks red with cold
your breath visible as it rises
over water tumbling over rock

3.
a shooting star
as seen from ridgetop,
cornfields contouring out
from either side of you
this shooting star
blazing long and bright enough
for you to point
and find the words *look! a meteor!*
and get them out of your mouth
and still, it shimmers there,
carving its way
across country-dark sky

4.
the calendar you keep
just to fill in the little celebrations
of daily magic:
the first robins,
the dried oak leaves that have hung on all winter
twisting in the brace-yourself winds,
the raccoon prints in the mud

5.
the names of colors
you can come up with
for each sunset sky
for instance:
purple pearlescent haze,
grandma's face powder
1979 prom dress
neo-neapolitan (blueberry lavender,
fuschia strawberry, and cool vanilla)
or too hot and too pink to name

6.
the winter wind with snow in it
kicked up to thirty miles per hour
smudging the landscape
(cow pasture, soy fields)
into a greybluewhite blur
and the curved icicles
slanting in the direction of the gusts
hanging from the neighbor's gutters
and you, standing warm at the window
laughing out into the brutal
icicle-bending air

7.
the pine needle tea
steeping on the porch railing
in a glass pitcher under May's already-hot sun
clear water slowly
turning peachgold

8.
the moonlight on the Mississippi gone blue with sky
refracting, reflecting, glowing out
towards you
as it rises over the wide and shimmering waters

9.
baptism you say about
our heads under the smallest waterfall
at the limestone sand cave
that we hiked down through the ferns
and birches to get to,
the cool drips running over
our scalps
our throats
our saltsweaty necks

Bicycling the Driftless

Margot Higgins

I bicycle the Driftless to embody the shape of it. I bicycle to view the expanse of rolling hills from a ridgeline. I want to feel the swing of my hips when I descend a curve, the burn in my thighs when I climb, the expanse of breath in my lungs when I reach the top. I like the way these hills make my heart beat fast.

As one friend put it, the topography here is like a crumpled-up piece of paper with rounded edges. The roads are anomalous, thinner, windier, and steeper than others I have known. Physical exertion on two wheels sharpens my ability to absorb my surroundings. I am more apt to notice the subtle shifts in daily temperatures, the approximate speed of strong headwinds that blow against me, or the tailwinds that propel me forward at thirty-five miles an hour.

Bicycling provides another realm for reflection. In an embodied thinking space, I make it an office, ruminating on lesson plans for my environmental studies students. I consider revisions to the journal article I am working on or the logistics of a field trip I am organizing. On other days, I am also driftless and let my mind wander around each bend in the road to see where it goes. I reflect on the loved ones in my life and the space I have found as a home for this place and time.

After an early April thaw, I hit an unfamiliar pothole that throws off my balance. A new stretch of gravel surprises me, and I skid. I am aware that ice will likely make the roads slippery again in a place where winter's memory remains strong. The growing season begins, and longer days infuse me with insatiable energy, understanding that in late summer I will see it reverse. I repeat some of my favorite routes. It is important to travel in both directions to see where one has been. What has changed in me since the year before? Bicycling the landscape offers me a reference point.

I am grateful that *this* is my drug of choice, countering stress, infusing my cells with oxygen, and often making me tipsy with endorphins. Spinning two thin wheels through space steadies me. Once I had repeated dizzy spells following seizures, and the bicycle grounded me physically and inwardly.

Sometimes I want to ride slowly—do it on a bicycle instead of in an Outback. This leads to less expedition and more contemplation. I want to look at the expanse of the land from a ridgetop and cut worries down to size, make problems more lucid, more tangible.

I see a barred owl clinging to a withered stalk of milkweed. I pull over to spend time with her here, lock eyes, look down, and see what she might be eating. This one doesn't flinch when a black Dodge Ram with a tractor in pull zigzags by. But still, it disappears in a few minutes, chasing something my eyes will never see. Following that track, I am slightly edged into the other lane. I understand that I shouldn't pull over here where the roads are windy and filled with the invisible. Deer leap in front of you before you can see them. I hit a turkey once.

I often share the road with Amish buggies, who click and clack behind me, pulling over politely to let me pass. Before them, colonial settlers were in this area, and before them, it was a place for tribal nations to converge, where trails followed water drainages that preceded the boundaries imposed by our paved road system. Many of the roads I travel follow the same path. It's an area with a high number of burial mounds, sometimes on the agricultural fields I pass. I've been curious about how these communities get sewn up together and the ways people put them into a story. I consider what it means to belong, how to stay connected to my circle of lifelong friends and family who live afar. Having lived all over the map, I think about how to be more embedded here. I have some holes. Places that need patching. Roots ready to grow.

Just after I moved to La Crosse, I was invited on a blind date in Viroqua. I did not hesitate to arrive on two wheels as an introduction to the person I feel I am—one who prefers to travel by their own power. I failed to factor in three substantial climbs involved on the journey. Luckily, that person seemed to understand why I was over an hour late, and they kindly drove me home after dark to avoid a rather perilous ride home on cavernous rural roads.

Riding to Viroqua, I was mesmerized for the first time by the pattern and contour lines of the cornfields. That cropping technique was implemented in the 1930s to stop the rapid erosion caused by right-angled checkerboarded attempts to grow things in this region. I had read about the distinct history in Coon Valley of community-based soil conservation, which was the first experiment of its kind in this country during the Great Depression when local people, the government, and university researchers worked to create an alternative model for agriculture. That project helped to re-establish the world-class trout fishing streams and majestic scenery that attracts so many visitors to the area today. What would a contemporary version look like?

It is easy to forget that this area has been subject to unprecedented flooding over the last decade, with three hundred-year level floods. Homes are swept away. Cows drown. Livelihoods submerged. People displaced. I have had to re-route my ride several times due to an unexpected blown-out bridge.

Each flood compounds existing challenges in this rural and under-resourced region with a higher poverty level than the state average, limited access to health care, schooling, and decent-paying jobs. Services are spread farther and farther apart. Yet when floods happen, people in these small communities come together in the absence of state support. They respond to damage exacerbated by structural neglect. They come together to do the work of recovery and create channels for others to join the effort.

Down in the damp, spongy valleys, the trees look like broccoli. The Kickapoo River runs clear. I roll through the kale, cabbage, and potato fields of Amish farmers, plowed by draft horses. I pass greenhouses and maple syrup roadside stands, schoolhouses from the late 1800s. This is also an expanse of vast ecosystems governed by organic processes. Heavy industry coexists here with living traditional lifeways and people challenging the conventional food system with individual and community actions. Here, more small dairy farms have been able to hold on than any other part of the state. There is more organic food production per capita than in any other place in the country, next to California. And yet, large-scale feeding operations still are finding a way to creep in. I cough when I inhale a wave of fertilizer during spraying season. I hear anecdotally that more miscarriages follow this time of the year.

And yet, each day of navigating the labyrinth of hills offers the possibility of another route, a new direction to take. Sometimes I get lost. It is pretty much the norm for a Google map to wink out sometime on a ride in the Driftless. I purposefully try to design my bicycle rides neither as confrontation nor denunciation. I want to see crumbled barns, wave at my favorite granddaddy billy goat, attempt to identify new native plants that pop

97

up each week in the summer, the rapid flush of sugar maple leaves in the fall, ice-glazed cow parsnip as the days grow short. I want to hear the prehistoric call of sandhill cranes and the sound of the way water flows through this particular land. I wave at the enormous pickup trucks as they rumble toward me, and the driver almost always waves back. Every so often, we recognize one another. Those are the moments that sink me into knowing this place. I understand that some things aren't right here, and I know I can't out bike or catch up to all of them, but all of my sweaty cells know that one answer is to continue down the road in the last light of the day.

River Valley Morning

Christel Maass

I've returned to this river valley
for the peace—
to do nothing
but watch the light
on the pancake-rock hills
and listen.

Jays whistle in passing, crows cackle
from empty branches, and a vee
of honking geese points away
high overhead. I know
it's their off-season,
yet the cranes I patiently hope for
arrive, cut through the ashen sky, with calls
ancient like this land.

Mostly, this morning
I listen for the clip-clop of a horse and buggy,
wait for the black shapes to appear
along the snaking curves of the empty road,
turn into the next valley, disappear
into its snow-dappled folds
as another day—
this one my birthday—
rolls into time.

Overheard at the Amish Shop in the Driftless

Christel Maass

To get to Owen's place
go to the top of the ridge
after passing through the next valley
and turn right at the red barn
with the yellow flower.

What the Light Is Hiding

Tamara Dean

For some twelve thousand Wisconsin farm families, life changed dramatically in 1937. Electricity began flowing into their homes and barns. The Rural Electrification Act, which President Roosevelt had signed into law the previous year, provided utilities with money to install poles and wires where, until then, it hadn't been economical to do so. Most farmers were thrilled. One who lived near Janesville said of the power company crew: "I thought sometimes that they weren't ever goin' to get here. The organizers told us we'd have juice by spring. But we finally did get it, and by golly, I'm goin' to shoot the works." He showed a reporter every electric light in his barn. His newspaper profile reads like propaganda, and it might have been.

To persuade skeptical farmers—who, with the Great Depression fresh in their memory, balked at the prospect of a monthly electric bill—the Rural Electrification Administration (REA) mounted a forceful public relations campaign. Agents traveled across the country demonstrating electric appliances. Theaters showed a popular film, *Power and the Land,* which touted the benefits of electricity for agricultural operations and concluded with the line: "Things will be easier now." Part of the REA's campaign focused on convincing women. Electricity would give them lights, refrigerators, ovens, vacuum cleaners, washing machines, and irons they could plug into outlets. It would end their drudgery, the government promised.

But Jennie Harebo, a sixty-four-year-old woman from New Lisbon, Wisconsin, wasn't having it. After her town's rural electric cooperative set eight poles and lines on her property, she sawed down one of the poles and parked her coupe on the downed wires. She stationed herself in the car, armed with a shotgun and a hoe. Reporters called it a "sit-down strike," a "vigil," a "blockade." Her ailing husband brought her food. At dusk, she gathered blankets around her shoulders and cradled the shotgun. One night, two nights, three nights she stayed. A sign on the windshield read NOTICE: NO TRESPASSING. She allowed no negotiating. She entertained no tit-for-tat.

It's possible that Jennie Harebo, a woman of a certain age, was fed up with men's impositions. Now they were trying to force lines through her vantage, light into her dark. Maybe she wanted to hold fast to twilight powers— the wonderment, the wisdom, the privileged views. Maybe she was simply cantankerous in the original sense of the word, which is rooted in the notion of "holding fast."

What could she have seen in her three-night vigil? North Star, both Dippers, crescent moon's shine on the pump handle—the fixtures of haiku masters. Also, quotidian country lurkers and skulkers. Her night vision undefiled by electric shine, she probably saw scavenging raccoons, ambling possums, and scuffling skunks. Maybe a lynx's glassy stare. She heard more, too, than her city relatives in their wired homes with their humming lights and fans and blathering radios. She could have made out the lawyer's Pontiac approaching from ten miles away. She had plenty of time to aim her Remington out the driver's side window.

Eighty years after Harebo's stand, I took up wandering my rural Wisconsin property after nightfall. I longed for the sights that diurnal living denied me. Trail cams mounted in the forest or by the creek had offered only glimpses: beavers adding branches to their dams, stock-still deer staring straight into the lens. The cameras, I was sure, didn't reveal a fraction of the night's secrets.

On clear nights, I stood under the Milky Way's sprawling, splotchy canopy. I saw planets, constellations, comets, and once, a meteor afire and dying as it plummeted to Earth. The darkness of my rural township, an hour's drive from the Harebos' farm, was rare for modern times. In 2005, our town board passed a Dark Sky ordinance ("Whereas . . . whereas . . . whereas . . ." and so lights must be shielded, directed downward, calibrated, kept modest). Nevertheless, a yard light down the road, a sign at the corner bar, and the glow of a distant city interfered.

I sought deeper darkness. I found it at the nature preserve halfway between my place and the Harebos' farm. One night, a self-made astronomer and his telescope met me and others at the preserve for a moonlit hike. Inside the visitors' center, I discovered my friend Liz in the crowd, and we sat together. The occasion was a penumbral lunar eclipse. The astronomer began his program with corny jokes. He introduced his two assistants, women who knew the trails and would guide us on the night hike. He must have mentioned the alignment of heavenly bodies, how Earth's shadow would fall on February's full moon, the snow moon, once it rose. But I've never retained stargazing facts. I'm slow to make out asterisms. I can't recall which planets appear where and when and what temperaments the ancient Greeks assigned them. I merely love to bask under them.

We were all traipsing outside into the snow when the astronomer unexpectedly announced that hiking would be too dangerous because of the ice. Instead, he would talk to us during the half hour before the moon rose. The group groaned, and Liz and I looked at each other. Like the astronomer's assistants, we knew the preserve's trails, at least the main ones. We backed away from the others and stole into the darkness.

We padded slowly and quietly over the glazed snow, keeping our eyes on the ground, gathering scant reflected light from unknown sources. The woodland trail was icy only on rocks or railroad ties. In those spots we braced ourselves and reached out to steady each other. Soon we joined the wider trail, formerly the old state highway. There, the snow was ridged by snowmobiles' belts. As we walked on the crusted ridges, Liz told me about living in Dharamshala a few years earlier. I pictured her humid quarters in the mountains of northern India, the buildings' bright colors, the Buddhist pilgrims surrounding her. I sensed the peace she had felt there and nowhere else. Although I'd never been there, I shared her desire to return to Dharamshala. While visualizing that faraway place, I kept my eyes on my surroundings. Moving in the dark was a balancing art. I felt most adept when I looked out with a broad, allowing awareness, when I didn't fix on fine details or make assumptions about the terrain. Just as Liz and I arrived at the path's apogee, the clouds parted. The full moon rose orange, and as if cued by the shifting light, coyotes began howling.

What I have seen by the light of celestial bodies: rabbit prints as lavender shadows in the snow; bare, black elm branches waving; the red glow of varmints' eyes at the compost heap; stars in puddles and brooks; my lover's silhouette moving beside mine.

What I have not seen in the night and been surprised by: knee-deep muck; a snorting, thundering herd of deer; a frog on a door handle that I smashed under my palm as I hurried to get indoors during a rainstorm; a pickup truck without headlights barreling down the road and its drunk young man at the wheel who, after nearly running me over, reversed and asked, "Are you okay? Geez, are you okay?" in a tone that revealed his real question, *What are you doing walking out here after dark?*

To be moon-eyed is to keep your eyes wide open and to be awed. But to be moony is to be absent-minded, loony, or at least naive. With better night vision, I thought, I could steer my life toward more moon-eyed moments than moony ones. Maybe I could take in more good surprises than bad and live with heightened awareness, less delusion. Seeing what I'd been missing all along might grant me novel insights.

Humans are born with the ability to see in low light. But compared with that of other animals, our night vision is feeble. We lack the nocturnals' giant pupils (think *doe-eyed*) and their tapetum lucidum, a structure at the back of the eyeball that acts as a mirror, amplifying starlight into floodlight and reflecting it back onto the retina. Our natural night vision can be eased into—it takes a while for our sight to adjust to dimness—but in general, it can't be enhanced. Using lubricating eye drops or eating more beta-carotene, for most well-nourished Americans, won't improve it. Other habits, such as staring at computer screens or the sun, can degrade it. Unfortunately for Jennie Harebo and me and others past their physical prime, night vision also diminishes with age.

To compensate for human deficiencies, engineers developed night vision goggles during World War II. Now every optics store sells them. Some years ago, craving a clear view of the outdoors after sunset, I bought a pair. I stood on our deck, held the goggles to my face, and scanned the horizon. Deer in the field glowed an unnatural phosphor green. Nothing more. No portal opened to a secret world. No mysteries were revealed. In the years following my purchase, I rarely picked up the goggles when I set out in the dark. What I really wanted was something innate and unencumbered, a better version of what I was born with.

Scientists have researched ways of improving human night vision. A chlorophyll derivative called chlorin e6 has shown promise in mice. In 2015, Gabriel Licina and Jeffrey Tibbets, self-styled biohackers with a group called Science for the Masses, gained notoriety for trying the substance. A solution of chlorin e6 was dropped into Licina's eyes. Two hours later, he and others, acting as controls, were taken to a place where "trees and brush were used for 'blending,'" presumably an attempt to create a uniform backdrop. Licina and the control subjects were asked to identify letters or numbers on signs. The experiment was successful, apparently. Controls correctly identified the symbols a third of the time, while Licina did so 100 percent of the time. Afterward, he acknowledged to a journalist that the experiment was "kind of crap science." Without knowing the potentially harmful effects of chlorin e6, the biohacker had been willing to risk his everyday vision for the possibility of gaining night vision, if only for a few hours (the drops' effects wore off by sunrise). But Science for the Masses lacked sufficient funding to conduct the sort of extensive, ethical trials that more esteemed researchers require.

In photographs from that night, Licina stares at the camera like some mad alien, his eyes watery and opaque with their larger-than-life black irises—a consequence not of the chlorin e6 but of the oversized light-dimming contact lenses he wore. His eerie appearance and the report's description of him roving in a dark wood made me think that the young men had especially enjoyed the homemade horror film aspect of their experiment. Maybe they lusted after superpowers that would allow them to recognize and slay the dark's monsters. After all, night vision is one superhuman feat that's nearly achievable. Unlike time travel or leaping tall buildings, it's only just beyond our grasp.

"Darkness, pitch black and impenetrable, was the realm of the hobgoblin, the sprite, the will-o'-the-wisp, the boggle, the kelpie, the boggart, and the troll. Witches, obviously, were 'abroad,'" journalist Jon Henley wrote of life before artificial lighting in a 2009 article in *The Guardian.* Real monsters coexisted with the fantastical. In the London, Munich, and Paris of the early nineteenth century, thieves, rapists, and murderous gangs roamed freely. According to Roger Ekirch, author of *At Day's Close: Night in Times Past,* humans were never more afraid of the night than in the era just before gaslights illuminated the cities' streets. Murder rates then were five to ten times higher than they are today. And yet, Ekirch adds, "large numbers of people came up for air when the sun went down. It afforded them the privacy they did not have during the day. They could no longer be overseen by their superiors." Darkness made equals of poor and wealthy, servants and masters, women and men. Past sunset, oppressors needed artificial light to point out their symbols of country and religion, to run factories, and enforce conforming behaviors. For the less powerful, darkness and the ability to navigate celestially meant freedom.

Jennie Harebo's vigil attracted reporters and photographers from across Wisconsin, their cars lining the roads near her farm. The visitors, she said, treated her courteously. A deputy sheriff persuaded her to put down the shotgun. And the REA's lawyer finally relented, having decided to circumvent the Harebo farm after neighbors agreed to accept the poles and lines on their properties. The utility paid Harebo twenty-five dollars for her trouble and removed the eight poles it had installed on her land. "With nothing left to fight for," a newsman wrote, Harebo ended her vigil after about ninety-six hours. "Storing her formidable hoe in the woodshed, [she] claimed victory today." She abandoned her coupe, "her husky frame sagging a little with weariness." The crowd that had gathered to watch the three-day standoff dispersed. Another reporter mocked, "Ultimately, [the family's] need for kerosene lamps continued."

In opposing electricity, Harebo was a rare exception. Some farmers didn't even wait for the REA. Two decades before her blockade, men who once lived along the road between my home and the nature preserve were so eager to have electricity that they collected their own poles and wire. They used tractors, shovels, and muscle to run lines from the nearest village. Theirs was the nation's first farmer-led electrical cooperative. It functioned independently for twenty years, disbanding only in the early 1930s, when the state butted in and began interfering in its operations.

Although she opposed lines on her own property, I imagined that Harebo would have admired the farmers' refusal to comply with state regulations. As one farmer remarked on the public service commission's attempt to set his cooperative's prices, it "was a good example of the chair-bottom warmer's insatiable desire to run everything." In the years since I learned about Harebo's vigil, she'd become a heroine in my eyes. Here was a tough woman who had fended off the establishment. She had battled for her rights—to the darkness and the freedoms it brought her, to the preservation of her night vision—even if she was weary and sagging.

Standing on the groomed snowmobile route, Liz and I watched the full moon fade to yellow and shrink behind clouds. Then we left for the narrow forest trail. We picked over rocks and logs and a trickling, perennial creek. Farther on, we listened to our breathing and footfalls, nothing more. We found the meadow next to the parking lot of the visitors' center. Ahead, clustered around the telescope, stood the astronomer and part of the group we'd started with.

The clouds disappeared again. I looked up to watch the space station dash a diagonal across the sky. The astronomer invited me to view the moon in the telescope. "Lean into the eyepiece," he told me. "Don't touch anything."

Singled out in a close-up, the moon nearly blinded me. The penumbral eclipse, a subtle shading on the lunar surface, was too faint for me to detect. I kept my eye to the telescope only long enough to assure the astronomer that I'd made an effort. I didn't like the way the instrument isolated the moon. Without its complement of stars and planets, it was a flattened, vapid object. I felt as if I was ogling it but not really seeing it.

Liz took a brief turn at the eyepiece, too. Then we walked to our cars, agreeing to meet again for more nighttime hikes.

People soon will be able to choose better night vision like they can choose to eliminate forehead wrinkles. Professional scientists—not only biohackers—are working on it. In 2019, Gang Han and his fellow researchers at the University of Massachusetts Medical School announced that they had enabled mice to detect near-infrared (NIR) light by injecting nanoparticles into their eyes. After the injection, the mice could see phosphor-green shapes in the dark, as if they were wearing night vision goggles.

Not surprisingly, safety and security, national or personal, are often cited as reasons for such research and its funding. What if soldiers, for example, could see enemies after dark without the hassle and weight of equipment? In one article Han suggested testing the eye-injected nanoparticles on dogs next. "If we had a 'super dog' that could see NIR light," he told a reporter, "we could project a pattern onto a lawbreaker's body from a distance, and the dog could catch them without disturbing other people." As if criminals wouldn't dodge behind obstacles; as if police with their natural night vision could make out the perpetrators well enough to project shapes onto them; as if dogs wouldn't be distracted by all the marvels their new night vision revealed and dash away from their handlers.

The delivery method—an injection into the eye—also makes this night vision technique impractical. When I spoke with Han in 2023, he told me that his lab might soon begin testing a wearable device, such as a patch or contact lens, on humans. He imagined an application in which a security agent wearing a night vision patch could see details in facial recognition software that others could not. But for this, more funding would be required. Of the lab's many projects, night vision research has received the most attention in the media. But it has gained little interest from industry or government. People at the big granting agencies, such as the National Science Foundation or National Institutes of Health, Han told me, "can't recognize its importance in daily life."

Months after fixing Jennie Harebo's image in my mind, I found an article about her that I hadn't seen before. It included a photograph, likely taken after she ended her vigil. She looked nothing like the newsmen's descriptions. Although the image was dim from age and poor scanning, I could tell that her hair was curled and styled. She wore a buttoned-up overcoat with a contrasting collar, maybe fur. She struck a movie star's pose beside the coupe—jaw set, chin lifted, face turned slightly, gaze fixed on the middle distance. Her frame was upright, not sagging. She showed no sign of weariness after ninety-six hours in the car. Shotgun held at her side, she looked ecstatic and carefree. Seeing the photograph chastened me. I had allowed the newsmen's descriptions of Harebo to deceive me. I'd been willing to accept that she was crabby and exhausted from her ordeal. But the word *vigil,* after all, is rooted in *lively* and *strong.* Maybe she didn't consider it an ordeal at all. Maybe she relished the standoff.

Harebo's proud posture reminded me of when I lived in Lansing, Michigan, during college and joined friends to march down the middle of the street. We held posters or candles and shouted, "Women unite, take back the night!" We claimed our right to be safe from monsters in the dark—symbolically, of course. The real, human perpetrators were always about, day or night, visible or not. Who knows if our stand changed any policies. But it changed me. Marching to reclaim the dark brought me a sense of solidarity among women that school, work, and family had not. Even so, I thought as I studied Harebo's photograph, my efforts hadn't gone far enough. I hadn't fully imagined what we would do with our freedom after we won the night.

During the summer after our first moonlit hike, Liz and I took more late-night excursions to the middle of nowhere. What I saw with my natural, flawed night vision: shooting stars, swooping bats, slumbering farm machinery, and the lift and dip of a rare, blue-glowing firefly.

What I felt as I listened and shared more stories with my friend: a keener attunement, an ease among shadows, and the assurance of being fully seen—so much of what daylight's glare had been hiding.

Arms Full

Rachel Peller

We made our way through the thick brambles,
our arms covered in red lines going every which way.

Maya emerged as a beast of burrs!
Hundreds and hundreds of them
matted deep in her sheep-like fur, burrowed below the
    down.

I snipped away at multi-flora rose.
Rebecca sawed down patches of gooseberry.
I collected bags full of lush wild blackberry, another
    with plum and autumn olive,
heavy enough to squish themselves with the burden of
    their own dense weight in my backpack.

We wandered and watched, quiet observations of the
    woodpecker dents and the coyote deposits,
until it was time—as in, it just felt right—to sit on a
    ledge, drinking cold water out of a shared
thermos, our legs dangling over the limestone ridge.
I usually track my minutes.
But time was elusive today; it floated out of reach.
It could have been the woods, the sun, the wandering,
    the joy of being in her presence.
There was just my breath, and hers, and the dogs, and
    the breath of our home itself.

Down the whippoorwill trail, we meandered to the
    broad edge of the lower prairie, delicately
avoiding the sedge meadow that I think could absorb
    and consume me if the fog was just right.

We noticed the places the deer loved best, their cozy
    beds amidst the prairie we burned last spring.
Rebecca gathered swamp milkweed for me, collecting
    dozens of stems and trimming them one
by one into a bouquet I could carry.

Through the grass, past the spring, beyond the
    blackberry patch, over the bridge,
the sun was falling in the sky, casting shadows through
    Queen Cottonwood.
Our feet scraped against the dirt and gravel road,
Maya running between and ahead and back again in
    happy circles.
She—my wife, not the dog—described a scene for me:
    a moment in the future of our lives
together, the people we would share a meal with, the
    garden in joyful abundance, a place for
goats behind the old barn, a mural on the garden wall.

When I was eight, I dreamt of a husband and babies
    and a pretty home.
And here I was, one hand in hers, a family of friends and
    neighbors, a home of wild trees and
rolling hills.
Here I was, with a scratched-up arm full of wildflowers,
    a back well aware of the burden of
berries, a face just slightly sunburnt, and a dog who
    needed to soon be de-burred.
Here I was, in love, in love, in love
            with more than I dreamt was possible.

Driftless Heart

Rebecca Jamieson

It was a cold April day just before my fourth birthday when we stepped from our rusty sedan after the long drive to Wisconsin through Chicago traffic.

Quiet enveloped me. Every noise was enormous: wind billowing through the dark shoulders of the arborvitae that guarded the white house; streams of birdsong disappearing into the forest across the road; mooing from cows at the farm perched on the horizon, surrounded by bare fields.

My parents told me and my older sister, Sarah, that we'd start a new life here. They were glad to leave our dark basement apartment in Naperville, to escape the pancake-flat Chicago suburbs with their chemical-green lawns, miles of strip malls, and gray-pink nights that smothered the stars. But I loved the nearby park, where I caught glimpses of wildness as emerald-headed mallards glided over the pond. I looked forward to watching my older cousins play video games in the dark room full of joysticks and electrical cords at my aunt and uncle's house. I liked visiting Betty, the old woman who lived upstairs from us. I was eager to see whether she'd give us carrot sticks (gross) or oatmeal raisin cookies (acceptable), and if she'd catch the single clear drop of liquid that always hung poised on the edge of her nostril before it fell.

My parents said this new house would be better. It would have three bedrooms instead of one. My mother could plant the acre of land into the garden she'd always dreamed of, with vegetables, fruit trees, and flowers humming with bees. My father told us the land we'd live on was special. It was called the Driftless and hadn't been flattened by glaciers in the last ice age. It was full of caves, rivers, sandstone bluffs, and more wildlife than we'd ever seen in Naperville.

As I stood next to the car, legs stiff from the long drive, I saw myself reflected in the house's tall windows: a round-faced, pink-cheeked girl with scruffy blonde hair. I wore black Mary Janes with white socks, and my ankles were cold in the spring air. A fresh, earthy scent rose around me, and underneath the tall windows, I saw a miniature forest of blue stars—hundreds of tiny flowers I would later learn were called scillas. They swayed as if in greeting.

After the snug burrow of our apartment, the new house felt big and strange. Over the following weeks, my parents talked about it endlessly, my mother's voice growing tight as she asked how long it would take my father to remove the fake wood paneling in the dining room and the turquoise and orange shag carpet that covered every floor. But I was fascinated by the grains of sand in the pale blue paint that made tiny red dots in my fingers when I pressed them against the wall. Letters with cartoon animals paraded near the ceiling of the upstairs bedroom, and I hummed the alphabet as I ran my eyes from aardvark to zebra. In the cobwebby basement, we discovered a wooden barrel with carrots packed in sand. Looking at their withered nubs, I felt dizzy with all the lives that had come before me.

As the days unspooled into weeks, the novelty wore off, and I began asking when we were going back to Naperville. I missed our apartment and the comforting routine of our days. There was too much space here— too much silence. At night, the dark was thick as fur, and the house groaned like an animal. I refused to sleep alone, go upstairs alone, or use the bathroom without leaving the door ajar.

The days were endless. I didn't want to watch my father ripping the mouse-infested pink insulation from the attic or listen to the drone of Wisconsin Public Radio as my mother kneaded whole wheat bread. Sarah read books for hours, leaving me alone with my boredom. I wanted to go home. I flung my small body onto the yellow linoleum flowers of the kitchen floor, clenched my eyes tight, and screamed as if I were being torn limb from limb. The only neighbors within earshot came to the door, worried my parents were hurting me. I was hurt, but not in the way they feared. That move was my first heartbreak.

May came, greening the woods and fields, swirling white blossoms on the apple, pear, and plum trees that dotted our acre of land. At the Memorial Day picnic, I ate brats and potato salad from a paper plate, then ran across the grass with the other kids. I made friends with the girl who lived at the farm with the mooing cows. My parents talked with a group of gray-haired professors who invited us to hike on their land, including the miles of forest surrounding our house.

Slowly, the Driftless became my home. I grew strong exploring its woods and prairies. My days took the shape of its rhythm: hunting morel mushrooms in spring, picking blackcap raspberries in summer, watching oaks turn copper in autumn, and going sledding in winter. The natural world was vaster than I could have imagined. I grew to love the quiet that was not quiet but full of a thousand creatures, living.

Yet as I grew older, the city began to beckon once again. I beat against my parents and the walls of our house like a moth against glass, desperate for something bigger. Climbing to the top of our gnarled apple tree, I strained to see beyond the horizon. I waited for the moment each day when a teenage boy drove by in his red Firebird, one golden arm dangling from the window. My chest clenched with longing as I imagined my future driving with a boy like that, speeding toward a glittering city: somewhere loud, exciting, and a little dangerous.

Eventually, I did move away into that future. I moved to Portland, Oregon, and spent days in a bookstore that occupied an entire city block. I camped in the snow-capped Cascades and swam in the Pacific. I traveled to Europe, where I cried over Van Gogh's *Sunflowers* in Amsterdam, danced in Barcelona, and ate madeleines in a fourteenth-century monastery in Aix-en-Provence. I moved to Vermont to study creative writing. I ate maple creemees, saw giant puppets perform among wildflowers, and watched as the hills turned crimson and copper in autumn.

Throughout the twenty years I lived away from the Driftless, its memory grew within me, heavy with longing. It was not just the place where I grew up, but part of my body. The Driftless was buried within me like a sweet, secret tooth, a second heart. Absence grew into a pain worse than heartbreak, the land calling like birdsong in a dream. Until all I could do was pack up the years of my life, drive the thousand miles between us, and answer.

When I arrived in late autumn, the land was brown, and the sky was cloaked in gray clouds. The only people I knew were my parents and two old friends, and the pandemic had shuttered everything. Perhaps I had made a terrible mistake.

Throughout that lonely winter, I befriended the land. I discovered new natural areas and reacquainted myself with old ones. There were no mountains, oceans, or grand vistas. But every oak savannah, effigy mound, sandstone bluff, and meandering river made me tingle with joy. With recognition. Leaving had taught me many lessons, but now I was ready for a new adventure. Letting my roots sink deep into the Driftless earth.

What I Love About Where I Live, Driftless Region

Catherine Young

The missing glacial remains, making its name sound
as if it is unshackled; unanchored; unconstrained.
Rounded hills with their straight-lined limestone
hearts. I pretend they are mountains.

Water seeping from every crevice—clean, constant,
comforting as it sings, threading its way
to the Mississippi River.

All of the bright-green growing world rich in wild
foods to feed a pemmican heart with blackcaps
and hickory nuts and wild apples from trees
planted by deer.

Alphabet-lettered county highways passing former
dairy farms and the crossroads
where cheese factories once stood.

Golden gravel township roads that sing to my child-
heart of Yellow Brick Road and handcrafted houses
nestled against hills with their dreams, so innocent.

The librarian in Solar Town whose two-story palace
contains a coffee maker and glass elevator,
and she'll take you on a ride to the second floor.

The mail carrier, who still tethers each of us
to one another, weaving a township from which
most of the people have departed. The snows,
when they come, deep and thick to receive
my wooden skis; maple sap in buckets shining blue,
and on a clear winter day, the blue flames
from each step in snow; redwings and peepers
in March; snap peas in June straight from the vine;
barn swallows swerving in July; sandhill cranes
passing through; goldfinch and chickadee song all year,
but especially

the way the light angles
between these creek-carved
hills, each day of each year
of all the decades I have lived here.

When the August 29 Dragonflies Rise

Catherine Young

They come in the low, late August sun,
as if gold is what they are made of,
reflect the hay ground, cut clean, and ambering.
They come only now, when the sun drifts south
in the autumning year, day nearly done.
Dragonflies, by the hundreds—thousands—come.
Flash, and *flash*, they drone over and around you,
within reach, as if they stitch some invisible thread
between seasons, weave across and back as if
to mend your late summer grief.
All across the field, above, and in the distance
they rise; an echo of midsummer's fireflies.
Their sparks fill the air—
There! And there—and there!
Droning magnificent,
dragonflies sweep and dip
as if their only purpose
is to mirror August's burnished sun to you,
tell you, more than goldenrod can,
there is turning—and in the letting go
there's gold.

123

With Gratitude

C. Kubasta

This collection of voices wouldn't exist without a text from Keith Burrows of Republic of Letters Books, Mineral Point's fabulous independent bookstore. Keith messaged me about the approaching NEA Big Read grant deadline, wondering if Shake Rag Alley Center for the Arts would like to partner on *something*. My first response was panic—we were launching our catalog for the year, and I'd recently become executive director of our arts & crafts nonprofit after a whirlwind year that included a move, job change, end of a long-term relationship, and major surgery. But why not? As with every chance I've taken here in my new home in the Driftless, I've found people full of ideas, creativity, energy, and passion.

To that end, I'd like to thank everyone who contributed to this project (so many)! Our indefatigable grant partners include the Mineral Point Public Library, Little Creek Press, and Republic of Letters Books. With big thanks to Diane, Kayla, Kristin, Shannon, and Keith for your ideas and enthusiasm. Additionally, many area organizations supported programming throughout the year, including the Mineral Point Public Schools, faculty and students at UW–Platteville, the Driftless Writing Center, the Mineral Point Historical Society, the Mineral Point Library Archives, and the Southwest Wisconsin Cornish Society. What a pleasure to talk about books and writing and how we can share what matters through language.

We were so thankful to be able to engage with Kao Kalia Yang's memoir *The Latehomecomer*. Through discussion groups and conversations that came out of that reading, we learned about history and humanity and also about ourselves. Yang's reading was a highlight of our Mining Your Stories Writing Retreat this year, and that celebratory spirit continued throughout the weekend with a community of writers and teachers. On that weekend so many of us who worked on this collection were there: Sheree and Stormy (our editors!), Kristin (our publisher!), Heidi (our cover artist!), with friends and partners from all over the Driftless. None of this—anthology, retreat, community—would be possible without our fabulous staff, who makes things happen day after day with creativity, intelligence, and joy.

And for everyone who shared a bit of themselves— thank you. Maybe you told a story to a grandchild or niece; maybe you asked someone a question and leaned in and listened; maybe you sent in your writing to us— or maybe you were inspired to think about how we are shaped by migration and place and memory. I am thankful for the important reminder that place is both real and metaphor. As is home.

ABOUT THE AUTHORS

Hannah Adalance was born in Platteville, Wisconsin, to a Latina mother and an Ashkenazi Jewish father. She was raised running free in their back forty acres, picking gooseberries among the hills, winding creek, and spring-fed waterfall. She spent time in her twenties hitchhiking across America and is now a certified public accountant. Her poetry often explores the ways many things can be true at once. Hannah lives with her wife, their three fur babies, and their Roomba vacuum. Catch her latest blog post at www.hannahadalance.com

Jerry Apps was born and raised on a central Wis-consin farm. He is a former county extension agent and is professor emeritus at the University of Wisconsin–Madison, where he taught for thirty years. Today he works as a full-time writer and rural historian. He has created seven hour-long documentaries with PBS Wisconsin, has won several awards for his writing, and won a regional Emmy Award for the TV documentary *A Farm Winter*. He has authored more than forty fiction, nonfiction, and children's books on rural history, country life, and the environment.

Coleman is the founder of Shake Rag Alley's Alley Stage and has written more than forty plays, with productions in the Midwest, both coasts, London, and elsewhere. His writing has been featured in numerous journals, including the *Vassar Review* and the *Midwest Review*, and in numerous anthologies, including *Open Heart Chicago* and *Drama in the Time of Covid*. Coleman is the author of *Spoke*, named best memoir of 2014 by the International Book Awards. He is a proud member of the Dramatists Guild of America and, at the age of seventy-six, earned an MFA in Writing for Stage and Screen. Find more at www.colemanspoke.com. Previous versions of his play were staged at Forward Theater in Madison, Wisconsin, and Buffalo United Artists in Buffalo, New York.

Tamara Dean is an author of fiction and nonfiction. Her most recent book is *Shelter and Storm: At Home in the Driftless*. Her work has appeared in *The American Scholar*, *Creative Nonfiction*, *The Georgia Review*, *The Guardian*, *One Story*, *The Southern Review*, *STORY Magazine*, and elsewhere. Her essay, "Safer Than Childbirth," received a 2024 Pushcart Prize Special Mention, and "Slow Blues" was named a 2021 National Magazine Award finalist. While living in rural Vernon County, Wisconsin, she co-founded the community radio station WDRT and served on the boards of the Driftless Writing Center and Valley Stewardship Network. She now lives in Madison. A previous version of her essay, "What the Light Is Hiding," appeared in *The American Scholar* and is also included in *Shelter and Storm: At Home in the Driftless*.

Heidi Dyas-McBeth (cover artist) was born and raised in eastern Nebraska and studied art, women's studies, and human development at the University of Nebraska–Lincoln. After several years living at the edge of the

Shawnee National Forest in southern Illinois, she and her family settled in Wisconsin's Driftless Area in 1996— a unique and rugged landscape whose history continues to inspire her work. Heidi exhibits regularly at Rountree Gallery in Platteville, Wisconsin, where she serves as vice president of the all-volunteer gallery board. Her passion for sketchbooks led to the creation of the annual Sneak Peek Sketchbook exhibit in 2024. She recently joined the Shake Rag Alley Center for the Arts board and curriculum committee. An advocate for community-based art and creative resilience, Heidi continues to explore how personal experience and lived environment shape the stories we tell through visual expression.

Dale Easley is a retired emeritus professor of environmental science at the University of Dubuque, which he joined in 2005 after fifteen years at The University of New Orleans. He has been a volunteer math teacher in Kenya, a volunteer working on water wells in Haiti, and a Fulbright fellow in Qatar. He has taught geology, statistics, and environmental policy, plus led trip classes to dozens of national parks, New Orleans (geology and jazz), and Ghost Ranch, New Mexico (nature writing). Currently, he focuses on storytelling in science and creative nonfiction. His writing has appeared in *Folded Word*, *Blueline Magazine*, www.deadhousekeeping.com, *Contours*, *Big Muddy, Barstow and Grand*, and others. He loves to travel, write, and drink beer.

Sheree L. Greer (editor) is a writer, teacher, and arts administrator living in Tampa, Florida. She is the author of two novels, *Let the Lover Be* and *A Return to Arms*. Her work has been published online and in print at the *Bellevue Literary Review*, *Obsidian: Literature & Arts in the African Diaspora*, *Burrow Press Review*, *Lez Talk: A Collection of Black*

Lesbian Short Fiction, VerySmartBrothas, Autostraddle, Windy City Times, Full Bleed literary journal, *Current: An Anthology for Jackson, Mississippi, Windy City Queer: LGBTQ Dispatches from the Third Coast,* and others. In 2014, she founded Kitchen Table Literary Arts to showcase and support the work of BIPOC women and femme-identified nonbinary writers and poets. Sheree holds an MFA from Columbia College Chicago and is a VONA/VOICES alum, Astraea Lesbian Foundation for Justice grantee, Yaddo fellow, and Ragdale Artist House Rubin fellow. Her essay, "Bars," published in *Fourth Genre,* was nominated for a Pushcart Prize and was notably named in *The Best American Essays 2019.* Her essay, "None of This Is Bullshit," was published at *The Rumpus* and featured in "Memoir Mondays." Her latest Pushcart Prize-nominated work, "If You Scared Say You Scared," was published in *Bellevue Literary Review.* A founding member of the southern arts collective, The Rubber Bands, Sheree also curates an annual arts exhibition at the intersection of visual, performing, and literary art.

George Hesselberg grew up in the village of Bangor in La Crosse County. He has worked as a cheesemaker, cemetery gravedigger, bartender, sign painter, translator, night watchman at a Norwegian telephone company, stagehand, peanut brittle salesman, steel roofer, and, for forty-two years, newspaper reporter and columnist for the *Wisconsin State Journal.* He speaks Norwegian, studied philosophy and logic at the University of Oslo, Norway, and journalism at the University of Wisconsin. His work has been published in a collection of general columns, a collection of columns from the 1994 Winter Olympics, collections of children's stories, and, most recently, a collection of news obituaries, *Dead Lines: Slices of Life from the Obit Beat.* A previous version of his story,

"Wilma," appeared in the *Wisconsin State Journal.*

Margot Higgins is a professor in the Sustainability and Environmental Studies Program at the University of Wisconsin–La Crosse, where she instructs a bicycle history and politics class. She is also the co-owner of Driftless Bicycle Adventures. A previous version of her essay, "Bicycling the Driftless," was published in *Ocooch Mountain Echo.*

Christopher Hommerding earned his PhD in History from the University of Wisconsin–Madison, completing a dissertation focused on Robert Neal and Edgar Hellum and their work in Mineral Point, Wisconsin. He currently works in the field of historic preservation but continues to research histories of gender and sexuality in the built and natural environments. A previous version of his article, "'This Is Your Pasty': Queer Domesticity in the Wisconsin Driftless," appeared in the *Notches* blog.

Rebecca Jamieson is the author of the chapbook *The Body of All Things.* She is the winner of the 2024 Tupelo Quarterly Prose Prize, is a Pushcart Prize nominee, and her writing has appeared in *Entropy*, *The Offing*, *Rattle*, and elsewhere. She has been awarded fellowships from the Vermont Studio Center, the Fishtrap Writers' Conference, and the Spring Creek Project. Rebecca holds an MFA in Writing and Publishing from the Vermont College of Fine Arts, and she is the founder of Contemplate Create, where she teaches creative writing with a mindfulness lens. She grew up between Dodgeville and Spring Green and now lives on Ho-Chunk land in Madison, Wisconsin. When she isn't writing, she's cuddling her two cats, hiking, and baking. You can find her at www.contemplatecreate. com and on Instagram @rebeccabjamieson. Her essay, "Driftless Heart," previously appeared in *Reverie.*

Jesse Lee Kercheval is a poet, writer, graphic artist, and translator. Her most recent poetry collections are *I Want to Tell You, Un pez dorado no te sirve para nada*, and *America that island off the coast of France*, winner of the Dorset Prize. She is also the author of three short story collections: *Underground Women*; *The Alice Stories*, winner of the Prairie Schooner Fiction Book Award; and *Dogeater*, winner of the AWP Award in Short Fiction, as well as the novels *The Museum of Happiness* and *My Life as a Silent Movie*, and the memoir *Space*, winner of the Alex Award from the American Library Association. Her translations include *Love Poems* by Idea Vilariño and *The Invisible Bridge: Selected Poems of Circe Maia*, for which she was awarded an NEA in Translation. Her most recent book is the graphic memoir *French Girl*. She is the Zona Gale professor emerita of English at the University of Wisconsin–Madison and the series editor of the Wisconsin Poetry Series at the University of Wisconsin Press.

Kevin Koch is the author of *Midwest Bedrock: The Search for Nature's Soul in America's Heartland*; *The Thin Places: A Celtic Landscape from Ireland to the Driftless*; *The Driftless Land: Spirit of Place in the Upper Mississippi Valley*; and *Skiing At Midnight: A Nature Journal from Dubuque County, Iowa*. More of his work, including shorter works on outdoor places and photos, can be viewed at www.kevinkochdriftlessland.net. Koch is professor emeritus of English at Loras College in Dubuque, Iowa, where he taught for forty-two years, offering courses such as Writing the Midwest Landscape, Mississippi River Lore and Legacy, Nature Writing, Creative Nonfiction Writing, and Monastery Voice. When not teaching or writing, he and his wife can usually be found bicycling, hiking, or kayaking in the Driftless Area.

C. Kubasta (managing editor) writes poetry, fiction, and hybrid forms. Her most recent book is the poetry collection *Under the Tented Skin*. She is the executive director at Shake Rag Alley Center for the Arts in Mineral Point. She also serves as the president of the Wisconsin Fellowship of Poets and poetry editor at Brain Mill Press.

Andrea Larson was born and raised in Thorp, Wisconsin, and now lives in Ridgeway, Wisconsin. In between, she lived in Chicago and Madison. She is also grateful for short stints in Tigerton, Wisconsin; Phoenix, Arizona; and Umeå, Sweden. She is a social worker by training and is into all that promotes liberation of the self and others.

Christel Maass, who lives in southeastern Wisconsin, thinks of the Driftless region as her "heart land." Her poetry appears in *Bramble*, *The Solitary Plover*, the *Wisconsin Fellowship of Poets'* Calendar, the *Wisconsin's Great Waters* Calendar, the chapbook anthology *The Lake Is Mother to Us All: Poems Celebrating Lake Michigan*, and other publications. Her poem "River Valley Morning" first appeared in *Bramble*.

Curt Meine is a conservation biologist, environmental historian, and writer based in Sauk County, Wisconsin. He serves as senior fellow with The Aldo Leopold Foundation and the Center for Humans and Nature, as a research associate with the International Crane Foundation, and as an adjunct associate professor at the University of Wisconsin–Madison. For more than three decades he has worked with a wide array of organizations at the intersection of conservation, agriculture, water, climate change, environmental justice, and community resilience. Meine has authored and edited several books, including the award-winning biography *Aldo Leopold: His Life and Work* and *The Driftless Reader*. He served as an on-screen guide in the Emmy Award-winning documentary film *Green Fire: Aldo Leopold and a Land Ethic for Our Time*. His work has been recognized with a number of awards, including the Conservation Leadership Award of the Quivira Coalition and the Biodiversity Leadership Award of the Bay and Paul Foundations. In 2018, he was elected a Wisconsin Academy fellow of the Wisconsin Academy of Sciences, Arts and Letters.

Steve Alden Nelson was born, raised, and attended college in the Driftless region, where most of his eleven siblings still reside. He has written for stage and screen and is an award-winning actor. He now lives with his husband in Los Angeles.

Justin O'Brien is a retired advertising professional and writer who lives in Mineral Point, Wisconsin with his wife, Karen. His work has appeared in *Light Quarterly*, *Voice of the River Valley*, *Chicago Parent*, *Elysian Fields*, and other publications, and he was a contributor to *Contours: A Literary Landscape*, the *Encyclopedia of the Blues*, *Armitage Avenue Transcendentalists*, and *Base Paths: The Best of the Minneapolis Review of Baseball*. O'Brien is the author of *Chicago Yippie! '68*, an account of his experiences as a seventeen-year-old anti-war protester, and *Mischief and Mayhem*, an illustrated collection of poetry and light verse.

Jeremy Payne "JP" is Nova Yanu's daddy, life partner, joy-pository mentor, PhD student pause out, advocate, organizer, outdoor nurturer, critical contextualizer, cultural worker, and creator. A lifelong joy-transmitter, JP breathes life into social work practice and mental health service provider work through lectures, trainings, coaching, facilitation, and creativity. JP's roots are in Memphis, Tennessee, and Cairo-Future City, Illinois. He grew up in South Side Chicago and its suburbs before moving to the southwest Wisconsin tristate area in 2008. Holding a BS in Health and Wellness, an MSE in Adult Education-Human Services, and a Social Worker certification, he has over ten years of experience in educational and supportive services across diverse communities. He founded My Black Carrot LLC Mentoring Hub, a social change platform offering strong bi-directional partnerships and impact in the areas of cultural education, mentoring empowerment, social activation-transformation coaching, and outdoor nurture enrichment experiences (CMEST).

Rachel Peller is a queer mid-thirties woman committed to a year of energy and delight in 2025. Her ancestry is mostly German-Lutheran, Russian-Jewish, and very suburban, but she found a home at Rock Ridge Cooperative in rural Dodgeville with her wife and other beloved living beings. She believes in the power of connection and the strategy of curiosity and spends her time working with others to improve statewide collaboration across sectors and create a local community center at the heart of town.

Lynda Schaller grew up on a dairy farm in Wisconsin's Driftless region, free-ranging in woods and fields and listening to elders' tales. She has lived in the rural intentional community of Dancing Waters since its 1982 founding. There, she learns from the land, tends group process, and writes essays and poetry. A version of her poem "Inheritance" was previously published in *A Catalog of Small Machines.*

Stormy Stipe (editor) has published fiction, poetry, book reviews, and essays in such journals as *The Missouri Review*, *The Texas Review*, *American Book Review*, and *The Walrus*. She earned her doctorate from the Creative Writing Program at the University of Houston, her MFA from Sarah Lawrence College, and her BA from Stephens College in Columbia, Missouri. She teaches literature and creative writing at the University of Wisconsin–Platteville.

Jacquelyn Thomas returned home to the Driftless Area of Wisconsin after living more than thirty years in a Madison housing project where she served as director of an on-site community learning center. She has been awarded prizes for poetry and fiction by the Wisconsin Academy of Sciences, Arts and Letters. Her nonfiction work appears in *Proximity* magazine, where it was nominated for a Pushcart Prize, and *Fourth Genre* as runner-up in the Michael Steinberg Memorial Essay Contest.

Denise Thornton is an environmental journalist who has written for newspapers including the *Isthmus*, the *Chicago Tribune*, the *South Bend Tribune*, and is currently writing for The Aldo Leopold Foundation. She and her husband fell in love with the Driftless terrain on their first date and, many years later, achieved their goal to become stewards of forty-four Driftless acres, where they built their green dream home and poured themselves into the restoration of the surrounding prairie and woodland. Learn more about their efforts and discoveries at Denise's blog, *Digging in the Driftless*.

Franciszka Voeltz writes poems to go on a portable typewriter for magnificent strangers and has been facilitating community writing events and workshops for twenty years. Voeltz's chapbook *8 August* is available from Vegetarian Alcoholic Press, and their work has appeared in journals including *Dark Mountain, Analecta Literary Journal*, and *Adrienne*. Voeltz is a Springboard for the Arts Rural Regenerator fellow and recipient of other poetry fellowships, including those granted by the Helene Wurlitzer Foundation, Santa Fe Art Institute, and Art Farm. Franciszka earned an MFA in Writing from the University of California, San Diego, and currently writes and grows food in rural southwest Wisconsin. Their poem, "to those everywhere else," has previously been published in *Contours: A Literary Landscape*.

Catherine Young is a disabled writer and performing artist whose work is infused with a keen sense of place. A Wisconsin Poet Laureate finalist, Catherine is the author of the ecopoetry collection *Geosmin*, which won a Midwest Book Award, and the environmental memoir *Black Diamonds: A Childhood Colored by Coal*. Her work appears internationally and nationally in literary journals and anthologies, including *The Driftless Reader*, and her work has been nominated for Pushcart Prize. With artist Stephanie Motz, she created the freely distributed broadside "Invocation: Call It Home" to celebrate place and encourage ekphrasis. She leads writing workshops and records the weekly *Landward* podcast. Rooted in farm life, Catherine lives with her family in Wisconsin, where she is in love with meandering streams. She holds concern for water and deeply believes in the use of story and art as tools for transforming the world. Find more at www.catherineyoungwriter.com. Her poem, "What I Love About Where I Live, Driftless Region" previously appeared in her book *Geosmin*.

Printed in the United States
by Baker & Taylor Publisher Services